To

_____

From

_____

Date

_____

His Footsteps, My Pathway

© 2007 Roy Lessin

© 2007 Christian Art Gifts, RSA
    Christian Art Gifts Inc., IL, USA

Designed by Christian Art Gifts

Unless otherwise indicated, all Scripture quotations are taken from the *Holy Bible*, New International Version®. NIV®. Copyright © 1973, 1978, 1984 by International Bible Society. Used by permission of Zondervan Publishing House. All rights reserved.

Scripture quotations marked NLT are taken from the *Holy Bible*, New Living Translation, first edition, copyright © 1996. Used by permission of Tyndale House Publishers, Inc., Carol Stream, Illinois 60188. All rights reserved.

Scripture taken from the *Holy Bible*, King James Version. Copyright © 1962 by The Zondervan Corporation. Used by permission.

Scripture quotations marked NASB are taken from the *New American Standard Bible*. Copyright © The Lockman Foundation 1960, 1962, 1963, 1971, 1972, 1973, 1975, 1977. Used by permission.

Scripture quotations taken from the *Holy Bible*, New King James Version. Copyright © 1979, 1980, 1982 by Thomas Nelson Publishers, Inc. Used by permission. All rights reserved.

Scripture quotations marked ICB are taken from the International Children's Bible®. Copyright © 1986, 1988, 1999 by Thomas Nelson, Inc. Used by permission. All rights reserved.

Scripture quotations from THE MESSAGE. Copyright © by Eugene H. Peterson, 1993, 1994, 1995. Used by permission of NavPress Publishing Group.

Printed in China

ISBN 978-1-86920-836-3

07 08 09 10 11 12 13 14 15 16 – 10 9 8 7 6 5 4 3 2 1

ONE-MINUTE DEVOTIONS

His
FOOTSTEPS,
MY
PATHWAY

ROY LESSIN

christian
art gifts®

Dedication

This book is dedicated to my brother, Don, who lived for Jesus with all his heart and served Him as a missionary in Mexico for over 40 years.

Through the years he was my greatest mentor. In all our visits, he never failed to impart to me the heart of God. His impact upon my life and spirit are woven, like a thread, throughout the pages of this manuscript.

Don left a legacy of radical love, radical obedience, and radical commitment to Jesus Christ. His greatest reward was to sense the gentle breeze of His contentment.

Roy Lessin

January

Righteousness will go before Him,
and shall make
His footsteps our pathway.

Psalm 85:13 NKJV

Following in His Steps

Righteousness will go before Him,
and shall make His footsteps our pathway.

Psalm 85:13 NKJV

The call of Jesus upon your life is always to follow Him. He calls you to place your feet in the pathway of His footsteps. As you do, you will never take a wrong step, make a wrong turn, move in the wrong direction, or wind up in the wrong location. What kind of footsteps does Jesus leave for you to follow?

They are the footsteps of a Shepherd, leading you to quiet waters and lush pastures; they are the footsteps of a King, moving you on in His authority and victory; they are the footsteps of a Guide who goes before you and prepares the way; they are the footsteps of the Holy One, who leads you into everything that is right, and good, and altogether lovely.

Following Jesus

He who says he abides in Him
ought himself also to walk just as He walked.

1 John 2:6 NKJV

What a high and glorious calling you have been given, to walk as Jesus walked. How did Jesus walk when He lived among us? Here are some of the characteristics: Jesus

- glorified His Father.
- prayed.
- pleased His Father and was totally dependent upon Him.
- only spoke what His Father wanted Him to say.
- only did what His Father wanted Him to do.
- walked in the anointing and the power of the Holy Spirit.
- went about doing good.
- said "yes" to His Father's will, and "no" to the Devil.
- walked on the roads that brought Him to needy people, to hurting hearts, to sick bodies, to bound souls, and to lost lives.
- walked with tenderness and compassion, and He was a servant to all.

Roy Lessin

Trust in God's Faithfulness

So if you are suffering according to God's will,
keep on doing what is right, and trust yourself to
the God who made you, for He will never fail you.
1 Peter 4:19 NLT

The best thing that you can do with your life, your work, your ministry, your time, and your day is to put it into God's hands, and leave it there. God doesn't want you to take back something that you've given to Him, and He doesn't want you to pick up something that He has not asked you to carry.

You can trust yourself to the Lord because of two convincing reasons. One is that God has made you – He is your Creator, He brought you into this world, and He keeps you under His constant care.

The second reason is that God will never fail you – He has committed both His *power* and His *heart* to you today.

The Perfect God

Blessed be the L ORD God, the God of Israel.

Psalm 72:18 NKJV

What an awesome God we have. What a mighty God we serve. He is all-powerful, all-knowing, and ever-present.

God is perfect – without flaw in His nature, without spot in His character, and without blemish in His beauty. There is no one like Him.

Think of it, God never makes a mistake, never does anything wrong, never makes poor decisions, and never gives bad counsel.

Roy Lessin

God's Wondrous Ways

[God] only does wondrous things!
And blessed be His glorious name forever!
Psalm 72:18-19 NKJV

God's name is glorious and His works are wondrous.
God cannot do anything that is not wondrous.
What does wondrous mean?

It means that God will only work
in your life in ways that are
splendid, magnificent,
superb, sensational, terrific,
stupendous, phenomenal, astounding,
fabulous, amazing, astonishing,
incredible, and miraculous.

A Loving Father

*Blessed be God, even the **Father** of our Lord Jesus Christ, the Father of mercies, and the God of all comfort.*
2 Corinthians 1:3 KJV

There is nothing more endearing than to know that God, the Ruler of the universe and the Creator of all things, is your heavenly Father. God wants you to draw your understanding of fatherhood by looking to Him and knowing His heart.

He is a loving Father who cares deeply for His children. He is the Father of all mercies, of all grace and kindness, and the Author of every worthwhile thing that comes into your life. All that you receive comes from His heart and out of His Hand.

He is also the Father of all goodness and tenderness. You can be in awe of Him, respect Him, appreciate Him, celebrate Him, delight in Him, and honor Him. Because He is your loving Father, you do not need to be afraid of Him.

Roy Lessin

A Loving and Merciful God

Blessed be God, even the Father of
our Lord Jesus Christ, the Father of
mercies, *and the God of all comfort.*

2 Corinthians 1:3 KJV

The mercy of the Lord means that a river of compassion is constantly flowing out to you from the heart of God. In your pain, sorrow, and suffering, God is there – bringing relief, quieting your heart, and lifting your spirit. God will never leave you without comfort, assurance, and hope.

No matter how great the problem, no matter how heavy the burden, no matter how dark the day, God's presence will be with you.

He will be there with a word of peace, with a touch of calmness, with a sure promise, with acts of kindness, with hands of healing, with songs of deliverance, with abundant grace, with tender care, with joys unspeakable, with peace beyond understanding, and with a heart of everlasting love.

His Footsteps, My Pathway

The Words of Jesus (I)

"No man ever spoke like this Man!"
John 7:46 NKJV

Jesus' words are powerful and life changing. He is the only one who can speak the things that your heart needs to hear.

- Only He who calmed the storm can say,
        "Do not be afraid."

- Only He who freed you from your burdens can say,
        "I will give you rest."

- Only He who is God incarnate can say,
    "I am the Way, the Truth, and the Life."

Roy Lessin

The Words of Jesus (II)

- Only He who gives you living water can say,
  "Come to Me to drink."

- Only He who shed His blood on the cross can say,
  "Your sins are forgiven."

- Only He who rose from the dead can say,
  "I am the resurrection and the life."

- Only He who has gone to prepare a place for you can say,
  "Do not let your hearts be troubled."

"I have come that they may have life,
and have it to the full."
John 10:10

God Comforts Us

[God comforts us] in all our tribulation, that we may be able to comfort those who are in any trouble, with the comfort with which we ourselves are comforted by God.

2 Corinthians 1:4 NKJV

In every trial of life, through every difficult circumstance, and whenever you are tested or persecuted, God comforts you. In times of loss and times of tears, in times of sadness and times of loneliness, in times of weakness and times of weariness, God comforts you.

- God comforts you with the arms of reassurance – holding you up and strengthening you to take the next step.
- He comforts you with the embrace of understanding – assuring you that He knows your heart.
- He comforts you with the touch of compassion – wiping away your tears and keeping you ever-close to Him.
- He comforts you with the words of hope – promising you that there are better things ahead.

Roy Lessin

Eternal Pleasures from God's Hand

*This world is fading away. But if you do
the will of God, you will live forever.*

1 John 2:17 NLT

Everything that is worthy of your time, attention, devotion, and affection comes to you from God. His voice will bring you healing words, His hand will give you good things, and His presence will give you eternal pleasures.

The world has nothing new to say to you that your heart needs to hear, nothing new to give to you that your heart needs to receive, and nothing new to demonstrate to you that your heart needs to long after.

For you, as you daily choose to follow His will, God's light shines brighter, His plan becomes more glorious, His love becomes more precious, His face becomes more beautiful, His treasures become more valued, His grace becomes more amazing, and His return becomes more anticipated.

The Only Truth

Love ... rejoices in the truth.

1 Corinthians 13:6 NKJV

God wants you to know the truth and celebrate the truth with each step that you take. In your spiritual journey, you have an enemy who will try and hinder the work that God is doing in your life.

One of the ways that the enemy will do this is through his lies. He will try and get you to question or doubt the truth of God. Here are a few of his lies:

- God can't be trusted
  (*The truth is, God is faithful*).
- God is against you
  (*The truth is, God is for you*).
- God really doesn't love you
  (*The truth is, God loves you with an everlasting love*).
- Your situation is hopeless
  (*The truth is, with God, nothing is impossible*).
- Things will never change
  (*The truth is, God makes all things new*).

Roy Lessin

The Path of Victory

*Then I heard a loud voice saying in heaven,
"Now salvation, and strength, and the kingdom
of our God, and the power of His Christ have come,
for the accuser of our brethren, who accused them
before our God day and night, has been cast down."*

Revelation 12:10 NKJV

As you follow God's footsteps you will walk upon God's victory path. The enemy has been defeated through the mighty redemptive work of Jesus Christ upon the cross. Victory is possible because of what Jesus has won for you.

Satan has been judged, and one day, his final sentence will be carried out. For now, you can apply the victory of Jesus Christ in the following ways:

- Resist the devil (1 Pet. 5:9).
- Raise your shield of faith and quench his fiery darts (Eph. 6:16).
- Take every evil thought captive (2 Cor. 10:5).
- Know the truth and speak the truth (Matt. 4:3-4).
- Walk in the Spirit (Rom. 8:1).
- Overcome the devil through the power and the covering of the blood of Jesus (Rev. 12:11).

Jesus' Victory is Your Victory

You are of God, little children, and
have overcome them, because He who is in you
is greater than he who is in the world.

1 John 4:4 NKJV

You have more going for you in Christ than what is coming against you in the world. Jesus came and destroyed the works of the Devil. Jesus crushed the enemy's kingdom under His feet. The Devil lost everything and gained nothing when Jesus died upon the cross.

Jesus reigns supreme in the universe, without a rival or an equal. Jesus is your victory, your strength, your power, your authority, your peace, and your wholeness. You are triumphant in Him, and more than a conqueror as you make His footsteps your pathway.

Jesus' victory is yours on weekdays and weekends, on cloudy days and sunny days; in every moment, in every location, in every phase of life; through every storm, through every trial, through every difficulty that you will ever face.

Roy Lessin

God's Tender Whisper

*I listen carefully to what God the L*ORD *is saying,*
for He speaks peace to His people, His faithful ones.
But let them not return to their foolish ways.

Psalm 85:8 NLT

God has something to say to you today, and it is good. There are a lot of negative voices that try to drown out the words that God is speaking to you. It is important that you quiet your heart daily and listen to the voice of your heavenly Father, and heed what He is saying.

His words are love-filled and life-giving. There is no voice that is sweeter or dearer. Listen to Him speak peace to you, hear Him comfort you and assure you of His presence.

God wants you to embrace every promise that comes from His heart to yours. Everything He says will build up your faith, lift up your spirit, and deepen your walk with Him.

God of Details

For thus says the LORD, who created the heavens,
who is God, who formed the earth and made it,
who has established it, who did not create
it in vain, who formed it to be inhabited:
"I am the LORD, and there is no other."

Isaiah 45:18 NKJV

God knows every star and has given them each a name; He has numbered every hair on your head; He sees every sparrow that falls; He forms every flower that blooms and every petal that grows. He sees every trusting soul, He hears every faith-filled prayer, and He knows every desire and longing of the heart.

God is a God of details and He watches over every detail of your life. He is watching over the details of His will for your life, caring for the details of your needs, providing for the details of your journey, tending to the details of your influence, overseeing the details of your service, and taking care of all the details that are necessary to make you into all that He has called you to be.

Roy Lessin

Walking in the Light

You must continue in the things which
you have learned and been assured of ...
2 Timothy 3:14 NKJV

As the world around you continues to grow darker, God wants you to walk in the things you already know – you are in spiritual warfare; God is on the throne; Jesus' victory is your victory; speak and live the truth while it is day.

Never forget that you have a Father in heaven who loves you and cares for you, a High Priest who prays for you with a heart of constant compassion, and a Comforter who is right there, in the midst of all you do.

The Holy Spirit is working in you the pathways of peace, the joys of God's presence, and the fulfillment of every desire within you that lines up with God's desire for you.

An Awesome God

But the men marveled, saying, "What manner of man is this, that even the winds and the sea obey Him!"
Matthew 8:27 KJV

Jesus has a way of amazing us. He says things that no one else can say, and does things that no one else can do. He is the Alpha and Omega, the First and the Last, the Beginning and the End, and much, much more.

Jesus is the:

- Messenger and the Message
- Morning Star and the Light of the World
- Root of Jesse and the Branch of David
- Servant and the King

Roy Lessin

Jesus Is ...

*"I am the bread of life. He who comes
to Me will never go hungry."*
John 6:35

Jesus is the:

- Shepherd and the Lamb
- Armor and the Warrior
- Sacrifice and the High Priest
- Vine and the Fruit
- Author and the Story
- Physician and the Cure
- Lifeline and the Anchor
- Promise and the Fulfillment.

His Footsteps, My Pathway

Work Heartily, As To the Lord

*"Therefore pray the Lord of the harvest
to send out laborers into His harvest."*

Matthew 9:38 NKJV

There are many reasons why the Lord's work should highly motivate you in your daily walk with Him.

- His work is always relevant to the needs you see around you
- His work has eternal importance
- His work is an expression of His heart and will bring Him glory
- His work is practical as well as spiritual
- His work fulfills His will
- His work bears fruit, builds faith, and brings life's true rewards.

Always remember that God has called you to the work you do, and that makes everything you do significant; God desires that the work you do be done as unto Him, and that makes everything you do meaningful; God provides the resources for the work you do, and that makes everything you do possible.

Roy Lessin

An Instrument for God

*Whatever I am now, it is all because God
poured out His special favor on me – and not
without results. For I have worked harder than
all the other apostles, yet it was not I but God
who was working through me by His grace.*

1 Corinthians 15:10 NLT

You serve a risen Lord and a mighty God through
the power of the Holy Spirit. Jesus can never be defeated and God can never fail. As you serve Him and
do His work, He is not dependent on your strength
to do what He asks you to do, but rather, He wants
you to be totally dependent on His strength.

Your hands, your feet, and your voice are the in-
struments that He uses to reach others. He works
through you, not because you are talented or edu-
cated, but because you are allowing Him to work
through you by His grace. God does not want you
to glory in the work that you are doing *for* Him, but
to celebrate the work that He is doing *through* you.

The Body of Christ

This precious treasure – this light and power that now shine within us – is held in perishable containers, that is, in our weak bodies. So everyone can see that our glorious power is from God and is not our own.

2 Corinthians 4:7 NLT

Part of God's glorious plan to reach the world and bless the lives of others is by working through His people, the body of Christ. Jesus Christ has chosen to send the Holy Spirit to live within you, so that you can respond to His leading in your life.

His presence in you is real and the results of Him working through you are powerful.

- Your hands can soothe as others sense His touch through you
- Your words can encourage as others hear His voice through you
- Your presence can bring peace as others sense His compassion through you
- Your eyes can bring hope as others see His light through you
- Your heart can bring healing as others feel His love through you.

Roy Lessin

God-Confidence

I am sure that God, who began the good work within you, will continue His work until it is finally finished on that day when Christ Jesus comes back again.

Philippians 1:6 NLT

It is a good thing to be a confident person if your confidence is in the Lord and not in yourself or in others. The world's message is "self-confidence", but the Kingdom's message is "God-confidence". Here are five things that you can confide in today.

- God holds you in His arms
  Each day He carries us in His arms (Ps. 68:19 NLT).
- God sustains you
  Give us this day our daily bread (Matt. 6:11 KJV).
- God covers you with His mercies
  His mercies begin afresh each day (Lam. 3:23 NLT).
- God pours out His love upon you
  Through each day the LORD pours His unfailing love upon me (Ps. 42:8 NLT).
- God will not fail you in any way
  The unfailing love of the LORD never ends! (Lam. 3:22 NLT).

A Kingdom that Cannot be Shaken

Wherefore we receiving a kingdom which cannot be moved, let us have grace, whereby we may serve God acceptably with reverence and godly fear.

Hebrews 12:28 KJV

Your confidence can stand firm because it is based upon something that cannot be moved, shaken, altered, or destroyed.

God's Kingdom will never crack under your feet or crumble before your eyes. You live in tough times, but you have a God who is almighty; you live in troubled times, but you have a God who is ever-present; you live in uncertain times, but you have a God who is all-knowing.

You can count on God today, even in the most difficult of circumstances, because His promises still remain, His grace still sustains, His peace still abides, His mercies still endure, and His love still upholds you with every breath you take.

Roy Lessin

A Prayer of Blessing

The Lord bless thee, and keep thee: the Lord
make His face shine upon thee, and be
gracious unto thee: the Lord lift up His
countenance upon thee, and give thee peace.

Numbers 6:24-26 KJV

May God's richest blessings be yours today. May His grace abound toward you, may His love cascade over you, and may the rivers of His goodness flow abundantly through you.

May He bless you with health in your body, joy in your soul, and peace in your heart. May He grant you strength for your daily tasks, wisdom in your decisions, favor in your labors, and provisions for your daily needs. May God's great outstretched hand of protection be over you and each family member. May He keep you throughout the day and bring you home safely from every journey.

Above all, may He bless you with His presence, keep your faith strong, cause your hope to remain steadfast, and keep your heart forever faithful.

A Servant's Prayer

Whatever you eat or drink or whatever
you do, you must do all for the glory of God.
1 Corinthians 10:31 NLT

Lord, this day is Yours and my life is Yours. May each step I take leave an imprint of Your glory; may each word I speak leave an echo of Your love; may each deed I do leave the fragrance of Your presence.

May my hands be an extension of Your mercies, may my heart be a mirror of Your heart, may my life be a reflection of Your image, and may my attitudes be an expression of Your nature to the lives of those You have called me to serve.

Thank You, Lord, for the privilege I have to be Your child, to be set apart for Your plans, to be called according to Your purposes, and to be used as an instrument of Your will.

Roy Lessin

Turn To God

*"Take My yoke upon you and learn from Me,
for I am gentle and lowly in heart,
and you will find rest for your souls."*

Matthew 11:29 NKJV

In our daily walk with the Lord there are certain things that we need to be aware of and guard against. We can carry things that God wants us to lay down, we can take up things that God does not want us to carry, we can neglect things that God wants us to observe, or we can look at things that God wants us to turn away from.

God has called you to turn away from your weakness and embrace His strength; turn away from your restlessness and embrace His rest; turn away from your heaviness and embrace His joy; turn away from your own understanding and embrace His wisdom; turn away from your own energy and embrace His power; turn away from your selfishness and embrace His love.

May You Be Blessed

May you be blessed by the LORD,
who made heaven and earth.

Psalm 115:15 NKJV

Jesus is the heartbeat of the Father's love, He is the beauty of the Father's face, and He is the glory of the Father's presence.

He is an endless stream of Living Water, a fountain of everlasting joy, and an ocean full of pleasures forevermore. He has so much that He desires to give to you, so much that He longs to be to you, and so much that He desires to do for you.

Today, may you be open to the wonders that He speaks to you; to the blessings that He pours upon you; to the promises that He affirms to you; to the grace that He multiplies to you; to the fellowship that He extends to you; to the love that He freely gives to you.

Roy Lessin

God of Abundant Blessings

*Jesus said, "I have come that they may have life,
and that they may have it more abundantly."*
John 10:10 NKJV

No one treats you more wonderfully than God. No one could ever be more generous, more gracious, or more loving than God is to you. His heart does not respond to you in guarded ways, His voice does not speak to you in limited terms, and His grace is never portioned out to you in limited measure.

God is always the God of *abundance*. He *pours out* His Spirit upon you; He *freely* gives you all things; He *abundantly* pardons you; He *generously* gives you His almighty power. God blesses you with *every* spiritual blessing that is in Jesus Christ. He makes you *more* than a conqueror through Him who loves you.

He makes it possible for you to do *all things* through Christ who strengthens you. He *always* leads you in triumph in Christ.

Pointing Others to Jesus

I call to remembrance the genuine faith that is in you,
which dwelt first in your grandmother Lois and your
mother Eunice, and I am persuaded is in you also.

2 Timothy 1:5 NKJV

Through your words, actions, attitudes, choices, and values, you faithfully provide the foundations of a godly heritage for those you love.

The heritage you leave should be one that motivates others to build their lives upon the same foundation that you have built your life upon. Your spiritual heritage will be marked by the ways you have followed God's footsteps, in the promises you embraced on your journey, in the steps of obedience you took along the way, in the ways you have allowed His character to be formed in you, and in the adventures of faith that caused you to trust Him completely.

Ask the Lord to make your life a sign post that will point others to His faithfulness, guide them to His heart, and lead them to His love.

Roy Lessin

Draw Near To God

*Let us therefore come boldly unto
the throne of grace, that we may obtain mercy,
and find grace to help in time of need.*

Hebrews 4:16 KJV

God is an ever-present help in time of need. There is not ever a time with God when He tells you that He will get to you as soon as He can, or that He is busy with other things at the moment.

His invitation is clear, "Come to Me for help, for I am your Helper." God's invitation is for you to come to His throne of grace, not to a throne of judgment; to come to a place where you can receive mercy, not to a place of condemnation; to come to a place of help, not to a place of rejection.

Whatever your trial, God sees.
Whatever your struggle, God knows.
Whatever your cry, God listens.
Whatever your difficulty, God cares.
Whatever your problem, God understands.
Whatever your need, God provides.

February

"I am the good shepherd.
The good shepherd gives His life for the sheep."

John 10:11 NKJV

Jesus Is the Answer

For unto us a child is born, unto us a son is given:
and the government shall be upon His shoulder:
and His name shall be called Wonderful ...

Isaiah 9:6 KJV

How wonderful and marvelous Jesus truly is. There is no one like Him. To every need He is the answer, and we can see His greatness through many different ways:

He is the baker's Bread, the quilter's Pattern, the homemaker's Guest, the gardener's Rose, the writer's Story, the musician's Song, the artist's Subject, the painter's Pallet, the builder's Foundation, the doctor's Physician, the explorer's Destination, the lawyer's Advocate, the architect's Cornerstone, the executive's Leader.

Jesus is the traveler's Highway, the navigator's True North, the preacher's Message, the intercessor's High Priest, the giver's Wealth, the servant's Master, the needy one's Provision, the thirsty one's Drink, the empty one's Fullness, the joyful one's Celebration, the seeker's Fulfillment, the worshiper's Object, and the heart's Delight.

Celebrate His love

*"I am the good shepherd. The good
shepherd gives His life for the sheep."*
John 10:11 NKJV

An elderly Bible scholar was once asked, "What is
the greatest truth that you have gathered from your
study of the Scriptures." His reply was simply,
"Jesus loves me this I know for the Bible tells me
so."

Isn't it wonderful that our simple faith can embrace such a powerful, all-encompassing, indescrib-
able love! Let today be a celebration of His love for
you.

Roy Lessin

Perfect Provider

*I will say of the LORD, "He is my refuge
and my fortress, my God in whom I trust."*

Psalm 91:2

Jesus loves you;
    no one could be more compassionate.

He prays for you;
    no one could be more understanding.

He cares for you;
    no one could be more thoughtful.

He keeps you;
    no one could be more protective.

He guards you;
    no one could be more watchful.

He leads you;
    no one could be more committed to your highest
good.

Follow in His Footsteps

You will show me the path of life;
in Your presence is fullness of joy;
at Your right hand are pleasures forevermore.

Psalm 16:11 NKJV

As you follow the pathway that is marked with God's footsteps, you discover that the various places He leads you in life will open up new discoveries of His character, nature, and love. Each characteristic of God that is revealed to you will bring you into a deeper joy and greater appreciation for all He is and all He does.

Because the Lord is your Provider you can know fullness; because He is your Treasure you can know satisfaction; because He is your Teacher you can know truth; because He is your Protector you can know security; because He is your Sufficiency you can know completeness.

Because He is your Warrior you can know victory; because He is your Comforter you can know peace; because He is your Father you can know love.

Roy Lessin

Serve Him

Whatever you do, do it heartily,
as to the Lord and not to men, knowing that
from the Lord you will receive the reward of
the inheritance; for you serve the Lord Christ.

Colossians 3:23-24 NKJV

God is the one who has called you to Himself, and He is the one who sends you out to serve Him. Your heart should be set on following His leading and what His Spirit directs you to do.

God may have you serve Him today in big ways or small ways. He may direct you to minister to one person or a multitude. He may ask you to speak or to be silent. As you serve Him today keep this following prayer in your heart:

Lord, the work I do is to glorify You, and that makes everything I do meaningful; the work I do comes from You, and that makes everything I do significant; the work I do is accomplished through You, and that makes everything I do possible.

Out of Your Love for Jesus

God our Savior showed us His kindness and love.

Titus 3:4 NLT

What should be our heart's deepest motivation as we serve the Lord? If it is for personal fulfillment and satisfaction then our lives will be empty; if it is for recognition and the praise of others then our lives will be hollow; if it is for personal gain or benefit then our lives will be shallow.

God is never pleased when our motivation in serving Him is for our own ends. There are many benefits and blessings that come to us as we serve the Lord, but they are the fruits of our obedience, not the reason for it.

Today, as you set your heart on the Lord, let each thing you do be done out of your love for Jesus, for Jesus has done everything out of His love for you.

Roy Lessin

Your Place in the Father's House

"In My Father's house are many mansions;
if it were not so, I would have told you.
I go to prepare a place for you."

John 14:2 NKJV

This world is temporary –
The powers that presently are,
will soon be the powers that were,
The wealth that presently is,
will soon be the wealth that was,
The fame that shines will soon be
the fame that has faded away.

Everything about
the kingdom of God is everlasting –
The joy you have will only increase,
The sweetness of the Lord
will only grow sweeter,
The beauty of the Lord's face
will only become more beautiful,
The glory of the Lord
will only become more glorious.

Jesus has gone to prepare a place for you. It will be
a place that is better than anything you have known.

His Footsteps, My Pathway

A New Spirit and a Tender Heart

"I will give them singleness of heart and
put a new spirit within them. I will take away their
hearts of stone and give them tender hearts instead."
Ezekiel 11:19 NLT

God has extended so much love, grace, and mercy to us. He has taken our cold hearts and warmed them, He has taken our empty hearts and filled them, He has taken our restless hearts and satisfied them, and He has taken our hard hearts and softened them.

God has taken our indifferent hearts and filled them with care; He has taken our judgmental hearts and filled them with mercy; He has taken our unforgiving hearts and filled them with grace; He has taken our self-seeking hearts and filled them with love.

Roy Lessin

A Servant's Heart

*"The greatest among you
will be your servant."*
Matthew 23:11

A servant's heart is from above
Formed in kindness, graced with love –
A heart that sooths each hurt and pain,
A heart that gives, and gives again;
A heart that's humble, a heart of care,
A heart of mercy, a heart of prayer.

No One Like God

"Who is like You, O LORD, among the gods?
Who is like You, glorious in holiness,
fearful in praises, doing wonders?"

Exodus 15:11 NKJV

No one is like God. His works and ways can be likened to many things:

- God is like an artist who paints every sunrise and sunset.
- He is like an author who has written His law upon our hearts.
- He is like a singer who joys over His people with singing.
- He is like an architect who has designed the universe and everything in it.

Roy Lessin

God's Wonderful Ways

More things to compare God's wonderful works to:

- He is like a lawyer who says, "Come and let us reason together."
- He is like an orator whose voice is as the sound of many waters.
- He is like a parent who attends to His children who are of the household of faith.
- He is like a wedding planner who is awaiting the marriage supper of the Lamb.

How great are Your works, O LORD,
how profound Your thoughts!

Psalm 92:5

The Nearness of His Presence

Yea, though I walk through the valley of the shadow
of death, I will fear no evil; for You are with me;
Your rod and Your staff, they comfort me.

Psalm 23:4 NKJV

Sometimes your walk with the Lord will take you through valleys. Valleys are narrow places. When God leads you through a valley He does not lead you into despair or fear. Rather, it is a place where He wants you to know Him more intimately.

In the narrow places of God's valleys you become closed in with Him. There is no room for others to walk with you through God's valleys; there is only room for you and God. It is a place where He comes near and tenderly draws you to Himself.

How sweet is the communion you have with Him, how dear to your heart is the nearness of His presence, how assuring and soothing is the comfort of His love.

Roy Lessin

On the Mountain and in the Valley

Show me Your ways, O LORD; teach me Your paths.

Psalm 25:4 NKJV

You learn things from God in the narrow valley that you cannot learn on the mountain top.

On the mountain top you learn that He is the God of glory and power; in the valley you learn that He is the God of all comfort and consolation.

On the mountain top you learn that He is the God who reigns; in the valley you learn that He is the God who bore your grief and carried your sorrows.

On the mountain top you learn that He is the God of justice and righteousness; in the valley you learn that He is the God of tender mercies and boundless grace.

On the mountain top you learn that He is the God of strength and wholeness; in the valley you learn that He is the God of healing and restoration.

The "Lunch Box" of God's Word

*Your words were found, and I ate them, and Your word
was to me the joy and rejoicing of my heart;
for I am called by Your name, O Lord God of hosts.*
Jeremiah 15:16 NKJV

A mother, who had a child with extreme food allergies, gave him these instructions on his first day of school, "Be careful not to eat food that others may give you. Be very sure to only eat the food that I send with you in your lunch box." That was very good council from a very wise mother.

We can learn wisdom from these same instructions as we apply them to our spiritual walk. Each day we are surrounded by things that are not good for us to feed upon. It is vital to our spiritual growth that we listen to what God is saying to us.

As our heavenly Father, He only wants us to feed upon what He has given us to eat out of the "lunch box" of His Word.

Roy Lessin

Embrace God's Greatness

Declare Your lovingkindness in the morning,
and Your faithfulness every night.

Psalm 92:2 NKJV

There are a lot of ways that you can start a day, but the most important way is to set your heart upon God and embrace His greatness and goodness. To embrace means to not only see His greatness and His goodness, but to affirm it in your spirit and proclaim it with your voice.

- Affirm that He is love and all together lovely.
- Affirm that you begin this day with your steps ordered by the One who only desires your highest good.
- Affirm that He is kind to you and that He will never lead you into anything that is hurtful or harmful.
- Affirm that He is everything that your heart longs for and everything you need.
- Affirm that He loves you with an everlasting love.

A Promise To Meet Every Need

*Wait on the LORD; be of good courage, and He
shall strengthen your heart; wait, I say, on the LORD!*

Psalm 27:14 NKJV

The God you trusted in the past
is the One who's faithful still.
Trust Him now, with all your heart,
to be working out His will.
There's nothing that you're facing
which takes Him by surprise.
All the things concerning you
have not escaped His eyes.

His grace has been your covering
through every circumstance,
Everything will work for good;
nothing is by chance.
Let your faith abide in Him
just like a mustard seed,
And you will find His promise true
to meet your every need.

Roy Lessin

Wait on God

Wait on God to do His work
in His perfect time and way.
The answer may seem slow just now,
but He will not delay.
One day you'll see the wisdom
that led you from the start,
was given by your Father's love
to draw you to His heart.

> *Wait for the Lord; be strong and*
> *take heart and wait for the Lord.*
> Psalm 27:14

His Footsteps, My Pathway

The Cross, My Victory

Finally, brethren, whatever things are true,
whatever things are noble, whatever things are just,
whatever things are pure, whatever things
are lovely, whatever things are of good report,
if there is any virtue and if there is anything
praiseworthy – meditate on these things.

Philippians 4:8 NKJV

When you hear words that are unkind,
When the answers you seek are hard to find,
Then think on the things that are true –

God is taking care of me;
Grace has set my spirit free;
The Cross is now my victory.

Roy Lessin

My Sacred Call

When others try to wreck your day,
When confusion tries to block your way,
Then think on the things that are good –

God will do everything right;
The Spirit's power is my might;
I see such beauty in His light.

When condemnation clouds your soul,
When inwardly you don't feel whole,
Then think on the things that are pure –

The blood of Jesus cleanses all;
Redemption saves me from the fall;
His glory is my sacred call.

*Commit your way to the LORD and He
will give you the desires of your heart.*

Psalm 37:5

Seek God Today

The eyes of the LORD are on the righteous,
and His ears are open to their cry.

Psalm 34:15 NKJV

Does your heart cry out for the heart of God? Do you long to know Him in a deeper way and follow Him more closely? Let your heart seek Him today with deep longing.

Jesus, precious Jesus, come and sup with me,
clothe me with Your righteousness, bring Your purity;
conform me to Your image, working deep within,
cleanse me with Your precious blood, wash me from
all sin.

Jesus, reign within me, and take Your holy place,
cleanse away the hardness that turns me from Your face;
renew me by Your Spirit, be my liberty,
bring to me a new song, and set my spirit free.

Roy Lessin

The Holy Spirit's Fresh Anointing

I have been anointed with fresh oil.

Psalm 92:10 NKJV

There is nothing stale or dull about your walk with Jesus. He is always the God of the moment and has something new for you each day. Included in the prayer that He taught His disciples are the words, "Give us this day our daily bread." Yesterday's food was for yesterday's need, yesterday's blessing was for yesterday's joy, and yesterday's grace was for yesterday's assignment.

Today, the Lord wants you to open your arms wide and embrace His new mercies. He wants you to open your spirit and receive the Holy Spirit's fresh oil and anointing. He wants you to drink anew of the living waters that flow from His throne, and He wants you to open your heart to receive a new outpouring of His tender love.

The Holy Spirit Is the One

"I will pray the Father, and He will give you another
Helper, that He may abide with you forever."

John 14:16 NKJV

What a treasure you have received in the person of the Holy Spirit. Jesus prayed and asked His Father to send the Holy Spirit to you. The Holy Spirit abides with you as an answer to Jesus' prayer.

The Holy Spirit is the One who drew your darkened heart to the light of Jesus Christ. He is the One who opened your eyes to the beauty of the Lord. The Holy Spirit is the One who guided your feet onto God's pathway, and He is the One who is leading you in the ways of righteousness.

The Holy Spirit is the One who is opening your understanding to God's truth, opening your spirit to God's presence, and opening your heart to God's love.

Roy Lessin

The Greatest Gift

*We are telling you about what we ourselves
have actually seen and heard, so that you may
have fellowship with us. And our fellowship is
with the Father and with His Son, Jesus Christ.*

1 John 1:3 NLT

The Father's greatest gift to you is His Son, Jesus
Christ. Jesus' greatest gift to you is the Holy Spirit.
The Holy Spirit's greatest gift to you is fellowship
with the Father and with the Son.

God's invitation to you is to look upon His Son
and to listen to Him. Jesus' invitation to you is to
hear what the Holy Spirit is saying to you. The Holy
Spirit's invitation to you is to allow Him to shine
His divine light on the face of Jesus.

The Holy Spirit wants you to see Jesus in all His
beauty. The Holy Spirit wants to shine His divine
light upon Jesus' majesty so that you can know Him
in all His glory. He wants to shine His divine light
upon Jesus' heart so that you can know the depths
of the love that Jesus carries for you.

Spiritual Blessings
in Heavenly Places

*Blessed be the God and Father of our
Lord Jesus Christ, who hath blessed us with all
spiritual blessings in heavenly places in Christ.*
Ephesians 1:3 KJV

God has given you the gift of Jesus. Jesus' gifts are
found in who He is and the blessings He gives.

Are you ...

- discouraged? Jesus will lift your head.
- weary? Jesus will give you rest.
- alone? Jesus will be your companion.
- looking for answers? Jesus will be your truth.
- hungry for God? Jesus will be your bread.
- seeking fulfillment? Jesus will be your answer.
- in need of hope? Jesus will be your future.
- looking for stability? Jesus will be your rock.
- looking for a reason to put in another day? Jesus
  will be your motivation.
- seeking purpose? Jesus will be your all.

Roy Lessin

Jesus Is Worthy

Worthy is the Lamb that was slain
to receive power, and riches, and wisdom, and strength,
and honor, and glory, and blessing.
Revelation 5:12 KJV

Jesus Christ is worthy of all your worship, all your praise, all your adoration, all your devotion, and all your dedication.

Jesus is the:

- Prize that is worth pursuing
- Way that is worth following
- Truth that is worth knowing
- Reality that is worth seeking
- Glory that is worth beholding
- Gift that is worth receiving
- Life that is worth possessing
- Goal that is worth gaining
- Highway that is worth traveling
- Promise that is worth trusting
- Joy that is worth celebrating
- Master that is worth serving
- Bridegroom that is worth waiting for.

Every Good and Perfect Gift

*Every good gift and every perfect gift is from above,
and comes down from the Father of lights, with
whom there is no variation or shadow of turning.*

James 1:17 NKJV

Think of all the edifying things, all the good things,
and all the meaningful things that are yours today
because of Jesus Christ.

He has answered your prayers, redeemed you,
washed and cleansed you, forgiven you from your
sin, delivered you from the powers of darkness, justified you, quickened you, given you peace, given
you a holy calling, made you alive in the Spirit,
brought you into fellowship with the Father, claimed
you as His own, given you access to the Throne of
Grace, made you righteous, sanctified you, given
you spiritual gifts, showered you with heavenly
blessings, given you life's true joys, given you an
eternal hope and brought you into His family.

Jesus made you an heir, and made heaven your
home.

Roy Lessin

The God of Peace

*Now may the **God of peace** Himself
sanctify you completely; and may your whole spirit,
soul, and body be preserved blameless
at the coming of our Lord Jesus Christ.*

1 Thessalonians 5:23 NKJV

God is the God of peace. Peace is a powerful signature of His work within your life. The absence of His peace is a good indicator that you need to examine your heart and allow Him to show you why His peace has been disturbed.

Every work of grace that God performs on your behalf, every work of His Spirit that He does in your heart, and every revelation that comes to you from His Word will be marked by peace.

Do you need to make an important decision? God's peace will be in the answer. Do you need to take a new step of faith? God's peace will move you on. Are you going through a difficult situation? God's peace will keep you steady through the storm.

Complete Sanctification

Now may the God of peace Himself
sanctify you completely; *and may your whole*
spirit, soul, and body be preserved blameless
at the coming of our Lord Jesus Christ.

1 Thessalonians 5:23 NKJV

What a blessing it is to know that God doesn't do anything haphazardly, indecisively, partially, or half-heartedly.

The work He has begun in you will be completed. He won't lead you halfway down the road you're traveling and then decide to abandon you.

Roy Lessin

You Are His

God won't fill you halfway-up with the Holy Spirit. The blood of Jesus doesn't just cleanse a certain percentage of your sins. God doesn't just allow some of His grace to abound toward you.

When God sanctifies you, it means that He completely sets you aside for Himself. He lays claim to every part of you. Your life is His, your plans are His, your times are His. He separates you from everything that defiles, to bring you into everything that is holy.

*"I have summoned you
by name; you are Mine."*
Isaiah 43:1

March

"I am the door. If anyone enters by Me,
he will be saved, and will go
in and out and find pasture."

John 10:9 NKJV

Jesus Is the Light

Then Jesus spoke to them again, saying,
"I am the light of the world. He who follows Me
shall not walk in darkness, but have the light of life."

John 8:12 NKJV

Jesus doesn't have light, He is the light. There are no dark places within Him. All that He is has been revealed for all to see. He is without flaw, blemish, or imperfection. His light is wondrous to behold and it is filled with more splendor, glory, and beauty than a thousand rainbows filling the summer sky.

The light of Jesus shines upon you with favor, kindness, mercy, and love; the light of Jesus shines within you with truth, hope, goodness, and righteousness; the light of Jesus shines through you with comfort, encouragement, compassion, and tender-care.

The light of Jesus shines upon your pathway, keeps you from falling, moves you in the right direction, and guides you safely home.

Jesus Christ,
the Eternal Son of God

Jesus said to them, "Most assuredly,
I say to you, before Abraham was, I AM."
John 8:58 NKJV

Jesus is not a past-tense Savior who did something for you once, but can do nothing for you now. He is not a future coming King who has no authority in the present. All that Jesus was, He is now; all that He is now, He will always be. Jesus Christ is the Eternal Son of God who became a man.

He is without beginning or end, yet He is the beginning and the end of all there is in time and space. He created the universe, the stars, the heavenly host, the earth, and everything on it. He is the beginning and the end of your faith, your hope, and your purpose.

He wrote the first chapter of your life, and He will place the final period at the end of your story.

Roy Lessin

Jesus Is the Only Door

"I am the door. If anyone enters by Me, he will be saved, and will go in and out and find pasture."

John 10:9 NKJV

There is no broadminded approach when it comes to entering into the life that God has for you. God doesn't present you with a variety of doors to consider. He doesn't say, "Go ahead and pick the door that looks best to you, and after you decide, I will support your decision and bless all that you do."

It is true that God does have a plan and a purpose for your life, but it can only be entered into through one door. Jesus Christ is that door. There is no other entrance. There is only one Gospel to believe; only one Truth to embrace; only one Shepherd to follow; only one Savior to trust; only one Lord to serve; only one Master to obey.

The Good Shepherd Cares

*"I am the good shepherd; and I know
My sheep, and am known by My own."*
John 10:14 NKJV

There are qualities that belong to the Good Shepherd that do not belong to a hired shepherd. A hired shepherd's main concern is himself, not the sheep that he watches over. The heart of a hired shepherd is revealed by Jesus when He says, "The hireling flees when he sees the wolf coming because he does not care for the sheep."

Jesus doesn't watch over your life because it is His job. He watches over you because He cares for you more deeply than anyone ever could. He demonstrated that care when He laid down His life for you on the cross.

If you are going through a difficult time at this moment, you do not need to wonder if Jesus cares. He cares more than you know, and He will never leave your life unguarded.

Roy Lessin

Jesus Knows You

*"I am the good shepherd; and **I know
My sheep**, and am known by My own."*
John 10:14 NKJV

When Jesus watches over your life it is not in the same way that someone watches a ballgame or a play. He is not a casual observer who passively sits back and watches the action taking place around you. When Jesus watches over you, it is as a Shepherd who watches over His lambs.

Jesus knows your exact location, your exact need, and your exact circumstances. Jesus, your Shepherd, knows how to deal with everything that you face, He knows how to handle every problem you encounter, and He knows how to shelter you from every storm that blows your way.

Jesus will not leave you on your own. His rod will be your protection, and His staff will be your comfort.

Listen and Obey

"Ye call Me Master and Lord:
and ye say well; for so I am."
John 13:13 KJV

To be Master means that Jesus is the teacher. To be Lord means that Jesus has absolute authority. Jesus is in complete control because all authority has been given to Him. Jesus is the perfect teacher because He doesn't teach you theory, but reality. Jesus doesn't teach information so you can have a big head, but He teaches transformation so that you can have a new heart.

As your teacher, Jesus wants you to listen to Him; as your Lord, Jesus wants you to obey Him. Jesus never gives you the option of choosing between the two. You cannot listen to Jesus' words and follow your own way, neither can you follow Jesus and not listen to what He has to say.

Roy Lessin

Abide in the Vine

*"I am the true vine, and
My Father is the vinedresser."*
John 15:1 NKJV

There is something that you can always be certain of as you abide in the vine – Jesus Christ and God the Father are deeply and intimately involved in your life.

The relationship of a branch to a vine signifies one of the closest relationships possible in creation. The branch is in the vine, the life of the vine is in the branch, and the Vinedresser is cutting back everything that will hinder it from bearing much fruit. Jesus used the relationship of the branch and the vine to remind you of how dependent you are upon Him.

Jesus doesn't command you to bear fruit, but He does command you to abide in Him. Fruit is the outcome of your abiding, and that fruit will always glorify the Father.

Prayer for the day

Commit your works to the LORD,
and your thoughts will be established.

Proverbs 16:3 NKJV

Lord in my life, work in me –

to plan with wisdom,
to guide with vision,
to lead with humility,
to listen with understanding,
to work with excellence,
to succeed in a way that honors You.

Roy Lessin

The Almighty Alpha and Omega

*"I am Alpha and Omega, the beginning and
the ending," saith the Lord, which is, and which
was, and which is to come, the Almighty.*

Revelation 1:8 KJV

You will discover what God has to say to you today
in the person of His Beloved Son. Jesus Christ is the
beginning of God's communication with you, and
Jesus is the final word when all has been spoken.
There is so much to be found in the person of Jesus
Christ that a lifetime of listening and learning cannot exhaust the subject of His person.

For any human to fully speak of Jesus Christ is
impossible. The artist could not find a canvas big
enough to contain His glory; the poet could not find
enough words in his vocabulary to fully describe
Him; the scribe could not find a large enough amount
of ink to record His magnificence; the author could
not find a big enough book to contain all His wonders.

God's Everlasting Love

The LORD has appeared of old to me, saying:
"Yes, I have loved you with an everlasting love;
therefore with lovingkindness I have drawn you."
Jeremiah 31:3 NKJV

Everything in your life that flows out of love has come to you from God. Everything in your life that is good has been initiated by God. Your life should be an ongoing expression of gratitude for all that He has done for you, all that He means to you, and all that He is becoming to you.

- Before you ever called upon Him in prayer, He made a way for you to come and receive mercy
- Before you ever turned to Him in repentance, He extended His grace to you
- Before you ever came to Him by faith, He drew you with an everlasting love
- Before you ever opened up your heart to Him in fellowship, He revealed His heart to you
- Before you ever reached out to Him for comfort, He embraced you with His outstretched hands.

Roy Lessin

Endless Spiritual Blessings

*"Blessed are those who hunger and thirst
for righteousness, for they shall be filled."*

Matthew 5:6 NKJV

Your daily hunger after God brings great joy to His heart. He celebrates your every step of obedience to His Word, your every response of faith to His leading, and your every expression of wonder for His ways with you. He delights in your pursuit to know Him more, in your desires to enjoy Him more, and in your longings to love Him more.

As you hunger after Him, you will find that His banqueting table is always full, that His portions are more than generous, and that His hospitality is beyond compare.

To hunger after Him means that you will never go away empty or dissatisfied. In Him are a thousand delights, a limitless supply of eternal joys, and an endless amount of spiritual blessings.

Praise God Always

By Him therefore let us offer the sacrifice
of praise to God continually, that is,
the fruit of our lips giving thanks to His name.

Hebrews 13:15 KJV

As you walk with Jesus day by day, you will find that your thankfulness to Him is a lifelong expression that flows from your heart to His. You, who have so little, have received so much, because He has been so generous. There are so many good things that are yours.

There are so many riches that He has given to you; so many answers to prayer that He has granted to you; so many kindnesses that He has manifested to you; so many joys that He has provided for you; so many mercies that He has extended to you; so many benefits that He has showered upon you.

Everything you have came from Him, and that is the reason why your heart can be so grateful.

Roy Lessin

The Awesome Wisdom of God

*Now unto the King eternal, immortal,
invisible, the only wise God, be honor
and glory for ever and ever. Amen.*

1 Timothy 1:17 KJV

God's wisdom is an awesome thing. Everything God made, He made in His wisdom. He put tiny walnuts on tall trees so that they would harmlessly fall to the ground, and He put huge watermelons and pumpkins on the ground so that they wouldn't fall at all.

You may not always understand what God is doing in your life, why He is leading you down a certain path, why He is allowing certain things to happen, but you can be certain that He is not making any mistakes.

His wisdom will not allow it. Everything that God is, He is eternally. His wisdom is eternal, which means He has never had a lapse in judgment, forgotten a detail, or miscalculated anything regarding your life.

Jesus, Lover of My Soul

"The Spirit that God made to live
in us wants us for Himself alone."
James 4:5 ICB

The relationship that you have with God the Father and with His Son, Jesus Christ, is jealously guarded by the Holy Spirit.

God, who has given Himself completely to you, wants you to give yourself completely to Him. In the book of the Song of Solomon we find these powerful words of devotion, affection, and love, "I belong to my lover, and he desires only me."

You have been called into a love relationship with Jesus Christ. He has wooed you, called you, and drawn you to His heart. He belongs to you and you belong to Him. He is the lover of your soul and He desires only you. He waits for you to respond to Him. He longs for you to long after Him.

Roy Lessin

Answer the Lord's Questions

*"Be strong like a man. I will ask you
questions, and you must answer Me."*

Job 38:3 ICB

As you walk with the Lord there may be times when
He will ask you questions. Here are a few questions that have been asked to others. What answers
would you give?

- Jesus asked, "Who do you say that I am?"
- Jesus asked, "Do you love Me more than these?"
- Jesus asked, "What do you think of Christ?"
- God asked, "Who will go for us, and whom shall
  I send?"
- God asked, "I am the LORD, is anything too hard
  for Me?"
- God asked, "Where are you, Adam?" (this ques-
  tion can imply, "Where are you in regard to your
  relationship with Me?")

Blessings of Goodness

The blessing of the LORD makes
a person rich, and He adds no sorrow with it.
Proverbs 10:22 NLT

Jesus is a wonderful Savior. He has given you richly and freely, all things to enjoy. Everything that comes to you from His hand is a blessing of goodness.

There are no sorrows attached to any blessing that He gives. When He provides, you are free from the sorrows that are brought on by greed, covetousness, striving, scheming, or manipulating.

Every blessing that He gives to you, whether spiritual or material comes with His peace and His approval. Even what He withholds from you is a blessing. He may withhold certain blessings from you because it is not the right time for you to have them.

There are also times when He will withhold a certain request from you because He wants to give you something better.

Roy Lessin

Life from God's Point of View

She ran and found Simon Peter and the other disciple,
the one whom Jesus loved. She said,
"They have taken the Lord's body out of the tomb,
and I don't know where they have put Him!"

John 20:2 NLT

It is easy to observe things with our natural eyes and form logical conclusions, instead of seeing things with our spiritual eyes and forming faith conclusions.

Mary observed all the physical evidence at the empty tomb correctly, but her natural reasoning caused her to come to the wrong conclusion. Since the body of Jesus was gone, she concluded that the body had been taken and moved.

The only way that you will be able to come to right conclusions about what God is doing in your life is to see things with the eyes of faith. There is no fog or blurry vision with the eyes of faith. Faith will allow you to see clearly and walk confidently, for faith sees life from God's point of view and does not operate on natural observation.

Passion and Zeal for God

Peter and the other disciple ran to the tomb to see.
The other disciple outran Peter and got there first.

John 20:3-4 NLT

God does caution us about doing things out of haste, acting too quickly, or making important decisions without first counting the cost of those decisions.

However, there is nothing in Scripture that cautions us to hold back our zeal or passion for Him. John's trip to the empty tomb was an all out effort. He held nothing back, but moved as fast his legs would carry him. Why the speed? He had to know what happened to Jesus. The Bible tells us that John was not only the first of the twelve to see the empty tomb, but that he was also the first one to believe (John 20:8).

Is there something deep within you that wants to know more of Him? Let your longing heart run to God with all your might.

Roy Lessin

New Light, New Truth, New Revelation

*For **as yet** they knew not the scripture, that He must rise again from the dead.*

John 20:9 KJV

One of the most exciting aspects of walking with Jesus is when He brings you new insights and a deeper understanding of His Word. It is like unexpectedly finding a large golden nugget or a rich vein of silver.

There are certain passages of Scripture that you may have read for years, but have not yet grasped their fullest meaning. In a given moment, the Holy Spirit can open your spiritual eyes to see something in those passages that you've never seen before. New light shines within you, new truth is opened before you, and new revelation dawns upon you.

Your faith moves to new heights, your vision of Him takes on new vistas, and your appreciation of the Scriptures grows to new depths.

Jesus Works in Supernatural Ways

Now when she had said this, she turned
around and saw Jesus standing there,
and did not know that it was Jesus.

John 20:14 NKJV

It's hard to imagine someone looking at Jesus and not knowing it is Jesus. Yet that is what happened to Mary. She didn't recognize Him because Jesus appeared to Mary in a way that was unfamiliar to her.

Is Jesus working in your life in unfamiliar ways? Do not assume that He will work in a certain way, or at a certain time according to your expectations. When you bring a need to Him, you may not always recognize how He is answering your prayer.

His answers may appear to be coincidental or circumstantial, but always remember that He often uses ordinary people and everyday events to work in supernatural ways.

Roy Lessin

Influence Others to Follow Christ

Be ye followers of me, even as I also am of Christ.
1 Corinthians 11:1 KJV

Throughout your life God has used others to influence you for the good, to follow His will, to seek His Kingdom and to know His heart.

God has used His people, the body of Christ, to influence you through prayer, through teaching, through ministry, and through example. You are not only a person who has been influenced by others, but you have also been called by God to be an influence to others.

How do you influence others to follow Christ? You influence others by following Him yourself.

Faith's Full Reward

For now we see through a glass, darkly;
but then face to face: now I know in part;
but then shall I know even as also I am known.

1 Corinthians 13:12 KJV

God always has something for you that is greater than what you presently know, what you presently do, and what you presently experience.

For now, you walk the pathway of a pilgrim, but one day you will actually arrive at your glorious destination.

For now, you live a life of faith and believe in many things that you do not yet see, but one day you will enter faith's full reward.

Roy Lessin

The Crown of Righteousness

For now, you are learning how to face difficulties and walk through hard times, but one day you will wear a victor's crown.

For now, you experience sorrows and shed many tears, but one day every tear will be wiped away.

For now, you are living by faith, but one day you will see Him face to face.

*Now there is in store for me the
crown of righteousness, which the Lord,
the righteous Judge, will award me.*

2 Timothy 4:8

God's Love Covers and Guards

Below is a paraphrased version of a powerful Scripture passage that will bring you great hope and encouragement as you reflect upon it.

Be persuaded, that neither death with its voice of fear, nor life with its many cares, nor the attacks of the enemy which falsely accuse you, nor things present with their pressing claims, nor things to come with their dark shadows, nor the height of any mountains that stand in your way.

Nor the depths of a great trial that you may walk through, nor any person or circumstance which tries to quench your joy or rob you of your peace shall be able to move you away, by even a single inch, from the Love of God that covers and guards your life.

Paraphrase of Romans 8:38-39

Roy Lessin

Outward Obedience
and Inward Rest

*May the God of peace Himself sanctify you completely;
and may your whole spirit, soul, and body be preserved
blameless at the coming of our Lord Jesus Christ.*

1 Thessalonians 5:23 NKJV

God has not called you to fragmentation, but to wholeness. He wants you to obey Him from the heart, not just from your will or your mind. He wants your obedience not to come out of duty or obligation, but out of your love for Him ("If you love Me, obey My commandments"). He wants everything you do to be in complete agreement with what He desires.

If you are traveling in your car on a highway that has a speed limit of 55 miles-per-hour, you may keep your car at that speed, but inwardly you may still be going 65.

Sanctification means that your inner-man is in agreement with what your outer man is doing. Ask God to bring you to a place of outward obedience and inward rest.

Jesus Christ, the Only Savior

Then Jesus told her, "I am the Messiah!"

John 4:26 NLT

The great proclamation of the Scriptures is that Jesus Christ is who He says He is. He is not a liar, a fake, or a phony. He is speaking truth when He declares Himself to be the Messiah.

Jesus Christ is the One the prophets spoke of, and He is the Anointed One sent by God. God will send no one else. Jesus Christ is God's anointed High Priest, He is God's anointed Prophet, and He is God's anointed King. Jesus Christ is the only one anointed by God to be your Savior.

No self-proclaimed messiah and no man-proclaimed god can save you. Only Jesus Christ can rightfully bear the names Wonderful, Counselor, Mighty God, Everlasting Father, Prince of Peace.

Roy Lessin

Do Not be Afraid

Jesus saith unto them, "It is I; be not afraid."
John 6:20 KJV

There was a time when the disciples of Jesus were traveling by boat to the city of Capernaum. It was night, and to their dismay, a great wind started to blow upon them as they rowed. The storm made their journey difficult.

Suddenly, Jesus appeared in the midst of the storm and spoke to them. As He spoke, Jesus gave them a reason not to be afraid (His reason was not that they would instantly be at their destination when He got into the boat, even though that's what happened). The reason that Jesus gave to the disciples was that He was there, in the midst of their situation.

Are you in a storm today? Jesus' words to you are, "Do not be afraid." His presence with you is the reason. Trust Him. He knows what to do to bring you safely through your storm.

The Bread of Life

Jesus replied, "I am the bread of life.
No one who comes to Me will ever be hungry again.
Those who believe in Me will never thirst."

John 6:35 NLT

Jesus makes an astonishing statement when He declares Himself to be the Bread of Life. When we think of bread, we think of something that accompanies a great meal, not something that is the meal.

When Jesus tells us that He is the Bread of Life, He is also telling us that we will never hunger again. It means that Jesus is enough! When we come to Him and partake of His life, we will never hunger after another savior to redeem us; we will never hunger after another god to bless us; we will never hunger after another teacher to instruct us.

Jesus' peace is enough, His presence is enough, His fellowship is enough; His atonement is enough, His Lordship is enough, His Kingdom is enough, His grace is enough, His mercy is enough, and His love is enough.

Roy Lessin

Eternal Realities
in a Temporal World

*Jesus said unto them, "Ye are from beneath; I am
from above: ye are of this world; I am not of this world."*
John 8:23 KJV

One thing that Jesus brings to our attention is the
importance of living in this world with our eyes
fixed upon what is above. A follower of the Lord
experiences eternal realities while he lives in a temporal world – he sees things that others do not see;
he hears things that others do not hear; he knows
things that others do not know.

A follower of the Lord believes in things that he
can't fully explain, he trusts in a Savior he has never
seen, and he longs for a place he has never been. A
follower of the Lord walks with his feet upon the
ground, while his eyes are fixed upon heaven.

He knows that all the things around him are
passing away, and that all that is before him will
last forever.

Jesus' Compassion (I)

*Jesus, when He came out, saw a great multitude
and was moved with compassion for them, because
they were like sheep not having a shepherd.*

Mark 6:34 NKJV

Jesus loves you,
    no one could be more committed;
He intercedes for you,
    no one could be more identified;
He cares for you,
    no one could be more compassionate;
He shields you,
    no one could be more protective;
He shepherds you,
    no one could be more watchful;
He assures you,
    no one could be more edifying.

Roy Lessin

Jesus' Compassion (II)

He embraces you,
　　no one could be more comforting;
He blesses you,
　　no one could be more generous;
He delights in you;
　　no one could be more affirming;
He calls to you,
　　no one could be more receptive;
He lives for you,
　　no one could be more available;
He speaks to you,
　　no one could be more intimate;
He provides for you,
　　no one could be more dependable.

"I am the good Shepherd;
and I lay down My life for the sheep."
John 10:14-15

April

Great is the LORD, and greatly to be praised;
and His greatness is unsearchable.

Psalm 145:3

Jesus Knows You by Name

Jesus said to her, "Mary!" She turned and said to Him, "Rabboni!" (which is to say, Teacher).

John 20:16 NKJV

Jesus knows you by name. When Jesus calls your name, you hear it spoken with a sound and a tone that you've never heard before. He speaks your name with tenderness, with compassion, and with deep affection.

It is spoken in a way that passes through your understanding and penetrates to the depths of your being. He speaks your name in a way that identifies you as His own. He speaks your name with the same love that He had for you when He laid down His life for you. When He speaks your name He is speaking as someone who knows all about you.

He knows your calling, your gifts, your desires, your needs, and what He has purposed for your life. Most of all, His voice reveals how dear you are to His heart.

Seeking what God Purposes You To Be

Not that I have already attained, or am already perfected; but I press on, that I may lay hold of that for which Christ Jesus has also laid hold of me.

Philippians 3:12 NKJV

It is clear from the Scriptures that God wants us to seek after Him. Sometimes we think that the word "seeker" applies only to people who do not know the Lord and are seeking the answers to life. A believer in Jesus Christ should never come to a place where he stops being a seeker.

Being a seeker means that you know God as a reality in your life, yet you are always hungering after a deeper intimacy with Him; being a seeker means that you know His love in your heart, yet you seek to know the fullness of its depth, its height, its width, and its length; being a seeker means that you have set your heart to lay hold of all the things that He purposes you to be.

Roy Lessin

God Is Seeking You

It is easy for us to understand our need to be a seeker after God, but it is quite another thing to realize that God is seeking after us. Two places in the Scriptures clearly point this out. One is found in Luke 19:10, "For the Son of Man has come to seek and to save that which was lost." God is seeking out lost people to bring them into a saving relationship with Himself.

The other is found in John 4:23, "But the hour is coming, and now is, when the true worshipers will worship the Father in spirit and truth; for the Father is seeking such to worship Him."

God is also seeking to find those who will worship Him in spirit and truth. His seeking heart will immediately respond when He sees you responding to Him and opening your heart to worship.

"So I say to you,
ask and it will be given to you;
seek, and you will find."
Luke 11:9 NKJV

God's Greatness Is Unsearchable

Great is the LORD, and greatly to be praised;
and His greatness is unsearchable.

Psalm 145:3 KJV

- God's love is so great that He cares about the smallest detail in your life.
- God's light is so holy that no darkness will ever come from His heart to yours.
- God's truth is so pure that it is impossible for Him to speak a lie to you.
- God's wisdom is so vast that He will never make a wrong decision regarding His will for you.

Roy Lessin

Fully Believe

*Then saith He to Thomas, "Reach hither
thy finger, and behold My hands;
and reach hither thy hand, and thrust it
into My side: and be not faithless, but believing."*

John 20:27 KJV

The Bible tells us about a man who was in desperate need to see his son delivered. When the man spoke with Jesus and heard about the importance of faith, the man said that he believed but wanted Jesus to help him with his unbelief.

Thomas was a believer in Jesus Christ, yet his faith struggled with the truth of Jesus being raised from the dead. It is possible for us to believe God regarding a particular area in our lives, yet doubt Him in another area. God wants us to become believers who *fully* believe.

He wants us to grow in our faith so that we can trust Him completely in every area of our lives, in every need we face, and in every circumstance we encounter.

More Than a Conqueror

But of Him you are in Christ Jesus, who became
for us wisdom from God – and righteousness
and sanctification and redemption.

1 Corinthians 1:30 NKJV

- Jesus not only wants you to believe that He has saved you from your past life, but that He can transform your present life and revolutionize your future
- He not only wants you to believe that He is your Savior, but that He is your Healer and can make you whole
- He not only wants you to believe that He is your salvation, but that He is your sanctification and can keep you pure
- He not only wants you to believe that He has destroyed the works of the devil, but that you can be more than a conqueror through Him
- He not only wants you to believe that He has done great things for you, but that He will work through you to bless the lives of others.

Roy Lessin

Complete Surrender

Thomas answered and said to Him,
"My Lord and my God!"
John 20:28 NKJV

The proclamation that came from the mouth of Thomas is one that Jesus desires to hear from each person who believes in Him. When Thomas spoke, he went beyond the understanding that Jesus was the Lord or that Jesus was someone else's Lord. He made it personal. He declared Jesus to be his Lord.

To call Jesus "Lord" means that you have completely surrendered to Him. Thomas declared complete allegiance to Jesus because He recognized His Lordship and His rightful ownership of His life.

Thomas didn't separate Jesus the Savior, from Jesus the Lord. In your life, the same response should be true. Jesus never told anyone that they could believe in Him as their Savior, but that they didn't have to follow Him as their Lord.

The Blood of Jesus Cleanses

For ye are bought with a price: therefore glorify God in your body, and in your spirit, which are God's.

1 Corinthians 6:20 KJV

The blood of Jesus Christ is powerful. It is His blood that makes it possible for you to be forgiven and cleansed from every sin. His shed blood is also the purchase price that has been paid for your redemption. What the blood of Jesus cleanses, it also claims. There is great blessing for believers when they recognize the claim that the blood of Jesus Christ has upon their lives.

It has been said, "God is ready to take full responsibility for the life that is totally yielded to Him." What a blessing that truth is! It means that you are not only completely the Lord's, but that He is completely yours. His righteousness is your righteousness, His strength is your strength, His peace is your peace, and His life is your life.

Roy Lessin

Truly Alive

*These are written that you may believe that
Jesus is the Christ, the Son of God, and that
believing you may have life in His name.*

John 20:31 NKJV

Jesus Christ is all about life, and believing in Him
means receiving His life. Jesus' life is everything
that is good, right, pure, and abundant.

His life builds up, it doesn't tear down;
His life restores, it doesn't destroy;
His life enriches, it doesn't deplete.

His life is true life. Jesus' life is not a false life,
a fake life, an artificial life, a phony life, a pretend
life, or a fantasy life. His life is not an empty life or a
meaningless life. His life is filled with purpose and
hope. His life is peace, contentment, and everlasting
joy. His life is not a passing away life, but a life that
is eternal. When Jesus' life is in you, then you are
truly alive.

Do You Love Jesus More?

*When they had eaten breakfast, Jesus said
to Simon Peter, "Simon, son of Jonah,
do you love Me more than these?" He said
to Him, "Yes, Lord; You know that I love You."
He said to him, "Feed My lambs."*

John 21:15 NKJV

When Jesus questioned Peter about his love, Jesus asked Peter, "Do you love Me more than these?" When Jesus used the word "these" what was He referring to? This text could be translated this way, "Do you love Me more than these things." What are the things in this setting? They are the fishing boat, the net, the large catch of fish, the fire, and the cooked meal.

The "things" represented Peter's trade, his security, his identity, and his ability to feed himself and his family. The question Jesus asks each of us is, "Do you love Me more than your job, your career, your comforts, your financial goals, your investments, or anything else that would make you feel secure in the world?"

Roy Lessin

No Comparison

*Jesus said to him, "If I will that he remain till
I come, what is that to you? You follow Me."*
John 21:22 NKJV

Following Jesus delivers you from the heavy burdens that can weigh you down on your spiritual journey. One of the things that He frees you from is the burden of comparing yourself to others.

When you shift the focus of your attention from what Jesus wants you to do, to what He wants others to do, you stumble and grow weary. Jesus does not want you to compare your journey to the journey of others.

When you follow Jesus with all your heart, you are not superior or inferior to any other believer. You do not need to puff yourself up or tear yourself down. You are who you are by the grace of God, and His grace is more than sufficient to enable you to fulfill what He has called you to do.

Enter God's Rest

For he who has entered His rest has himself also
ceased from his works as God did from His.

Hebrews 4:10 NKJV

God's rest is an abiding place for the believer. His rest frees you from all your efforts to make yourself righteous, to save yourself, and to try and earn God's love and favor.

You can rest because Jesus has done for you what you could not do for yourself. When He spoke from the cross and said, "It is finished," His words declare that there is nothing else that needs to be done to redeem your soul.

Roy Lessin

Jesus' Call To the Weary

*"Come to Me, all you who labor and
are heavy laden, and I will give you rest."*
Matthew 11:28

God will never require you to add an ounce of help or a few good works to make your salvation complete. Some Christians mistakenly think that the only thing God has to say to them is "Do, do, do."

Your Christian life doesn't begin with "do" but with "done." Jesus' call to the weary is, "Come to Me and find rest." Once you have entered into His rest, He wants you to remain there. From that point on, everything He calls you to do begins from a place of rest.

Your Highest Purpose

*"Abide in Me, and I in you. As the branch
cannot bear fruit of itself, except it abide in
the vine; no more can ye, except ye abide in Me."*

John 15:4 KJV

When the Lord calls you to abide in Him it means
that He wants you to be as near to His heart as He
is to yours. The beauty of abiding, is that it's a relationship of continued intimacy. It is an invitation for
you to allow His life to become your life; for you to
think as He thinks; for you to feel as He feels.

As you abide in the Lord you will sense His
heartbeat, be drawn by His love, be touched by His
compassion, be mentored by His voice, and be affirmed by His tenderness. He will become your ex-
pectancy, your delight, and your beloved.

As you abide in Him, you will discover that
pleasing Him will be your greatest joy, your highest
purpose, and your deepest satisfaction.

Roy Lessin

Already in Christ

*But of Him **you are in Christ Jesus,**
who became for us wisdom from God –
and righteousness and sanctification and redemption.*
1 Corinthians 1:30 NKJV

How does a believer in Jesus Christ find his place in Christ? The answer is a simple one. The believer does not need to find his place in Christ. The reason is because a believer *is* already in Christ. There is no need for you to ask for directions to get to someone's house if you are already there.

How did you get "in Christ?" How did this glorious and wonderful thing happen to you? God placed you there the moment you gave your heart to Him and were born again. Being in Christ is not a destination that you arrive at one day, but it is your home place – where you live, where you move, and where you have your being.

Slow Down and Listen

After the earthquake there was a fire,
but the LORD was not in the fire. And after the
fire there was the sound of a gentle whisper.
1 Kings 19:12 NLT

God does not want any of His spiritual children to be hard of hearing. He does not want any of us to be in such a spiritual state that He has to shout to get our attention. God's normal way of communicating and communing with you is in gentle whispers and in a quiet voice. It is the "still small voice" of the Holy Spirit that should be the strongest, clearest, and most endearing sound you hear in your spirit.

In order for you to hear His gentle voice you must lay down any lofty ambitions you are carrying, quiet down your anxious heart with all of its cares, slow down your hectic pace and packed schedule, and allow your heart and mind to settle down into God's good, acceptable, and perfect will.

Roy Lessin

Your Command Center

By my spirit within me I will seek You early.

Isaiah 26:9 NKJV

Have you ever wondered why God has given you a spirit? It is the most vital part of who you are. Without your spirit it would be impossible for you to know God on a personal and intimate level.

Without your spirit you could not have communion with God, enjoy His presence, worship Him, know truth, see the kingdom of God, have fellowship with other believers, or even pray.

God has never intended for the ideas that come from your own reasoning, the choices that come from your own will, or for the feelings that come from your own emotions to rule and control your life.

God has made your spirit to be the command center and the communication center through which the Holy Spirit controls your life.

You Are God's Child

*The Spirit Himself bears witness with
our spirit that we are children of God.*

Romans 8:16 NKJV

One of the most important things that you need to hear from the voice of the Holy Spirit is that you are God's child.

You will have no confidence to pray, to trust God for your daily needs, to claim His promises, to receive His covering and protection, to know His comfort, and to be certain of your place in heaven, unless you have the voice of the Holy Spirit telling your spirit that you are the Lord's.

Wishful thinking cannot give you this assurance. Your will-power and strong determination cannot produce it. Your family, pastor, or Christian friends cannot declare it. It is the voice of the Holy Spirit alone who can bring you this assurance, and His voice is all you will ever need.

Roy Lessin

The Exchanged Life

*I have been crucified with Christ; it is no longer
I who live, but Christ lives in me; and the life
which I now live in the flesh I live by faith in the
Son of God, who loved me and gave Himself for me.*

Galatians 2:20 NKJV

The Christian life has been called the exchanged life.
It means that God wants each of us to exchange our
life for Jesus' life. Here is a brief list of some of the
things we exchange with Him: We exchange our ...

- emptiness, for His fullness
- defeat, for His victory
- continued striving, for His perfect peace
- good works, for the abundance of His grace
- filthy rags of unrighteousness, for the white robes
  of His righteousness
- efforts to grind things out, for the flow of His
  Holy Spirit
- attempts to plan our lives, for His guidance and
  leading
- tension and heaviness, for the fullness of His
  joy
- selfish living, for His all-embracing love.

His Footsteps, My Pathway

Nurturing Love

"As the Father hath loved Me, so have
I loved you: continue ye in My love."

John 15:9 KJV

Your love Jesus, O Your love –
It is near to me, clear to me,
Every day more dear to me,
Jesus, thank You for Your love.

Your love Jesus, O Your love –
Like a flower unfolding,
Like strong arms upholding,
Your love strengthens me.

Your love Jesus, O Your love –
Like words unending,
Like prayers ascending,
Your love nurtures me.

Roy Lessin

Sheltering Love

"This is My commandment, that ye
love one another, as I have loved you."
John 15:12 KJV

Your love Jesus, O Your love –
Like rivers cascading,
Like the oak tree's shading,
Your love shelters me.

Your love Jesus, O Your love –
Like wings that are soaring,
Like dew in the morning,
Your love covers me.

Your love Jesus, O Your love –
It is near to me, clear to me,
Every day more dear to me,
Jesus, thank You for Your love.

Merciful Provider

Therefore, since we have this ministry,
as we have received mercy, we do not lose heart.

2 Corinthians 4:1 NKJV

God makes it possible for you to obey Him by supplying what you need:

- He is the One who provides you with seed so that you can have something to sow
- He is the One who gives you comfort so that you can comfort others
- He is the One who first loved you so that you can love others
- He is the one who has given you mercy so that you can extend mercy.

God commands you to forgive those who have trespassed against you, because He has forgiven the trespasses that you have committed against Him. You have been called to be a servant to others, because Jesus Christ came not to be served, but to serve and give His life as a ransom for many.

Roy Lessin

Doing the Father's Will

Jesus said to them again, "Peace to you!
As the Father has sent Me, I also send you."
John 20:21 NKJV

Jesus has sent you into the world in the same way that He was sent. Jesus did not send Himself out. He did not have a self-appointed ministry. He did not have a personal agenda that He set out to fulfill. He was not seeking a name for Himself or a reputation to glory in. He was not on a personal career path. He was not after power or wealth.

Jesus simply came to do what His Father in heaven sent Him to do. He spoke the words His Father gave Him; He did the works that His Father directed Him to do; He reached the ones that His Father wanted Him to reach. He had one main purpose, to glorify His Father.

Powerful Purification

*The priest will also sprinkle the dead bird's blood
seven times over the person being purified, and
the priest will pronounce that person to be ceremonially
clean. At the end of the ceremony, the priest will set the
living bird free so it can fly away into the open fields.*

Leviticus 14:7 NLT

Purification, as taught in the book of Leviticus, had two very powerful applications. These two applications were symbolized by two birds. This first bird, which symbolically represents a type of Christ's death on the cross, was slain and its blood was applied to the life of the person who was being purified.

Just as Christ's death on the cross never needs to be repeated, so the second bird was not slain. Instead, the second bird was set free to fly into the open fields.

The blood of Jesus Christ has not only cleansed you from your sins, but it has set you free from sin's power. How great is the salvation that Jesus Christ, God's perfect sacrifice, has provided for you.

Roy Lessin

A Part of God's Family

He shall be unclean. All the days he has the sore
he shall be unclean. He is unclean, and he shall
dwell alone; his dwelling shall be outside the camp.

Leviticus 13:46 NKJV

Leprosy is a disease in the Bible that is considered a type of sin. The consequences of leprosy were devastating, just as the consequences of sin are devastating in our lives. One of the terrible results of leprosy was that a person was isolated from everyone in Israel. In an instant, even the most well-liked person was an outsider.

When you lived in sin, you were separated from God, alone in the world, and outside the fellowship of the body of Christ. But thank God, because of the blood of Jesus Christ, you have been cleansed; you enjoy God's presence on a daily basis; you have been made a part of God's family; you have fellowship with other brothers and sisters in Christ.

The Ministry of the Holy Spirit

It came to pass, as He sat at meat with them,
He took bread, and blessed it, and brake, and gave to
them. And their eyes were opened, and they knew Him.
Luke 24:30-31 KJV

If you want to learn something about the natural world, regardless of the subject, it is easy to go to a library, take a class, or search the Internet for information. It is much different in the spiritual realm.

Biblical truth, spiritual riches, and heavenly realities must be revealed to you by the Spirit of God. It is the work and ministry of the Holy Spirit to open your spiritual eyes so that you can see and know the things that have been freely given to you by God.

It is a good thing for you to daily ask the Holy Spirit to give you new insights into His Word, and to give you a deeper understanding of who Jesus is and all He has done for you.

Roy Lessin

Covenant Promises and Blessings

*Likewise He also took the cup after supper,
saying, "This cup is the new covenant
in My blood, which is shed for you."*

Luke 22:20 NKJV

God is the God of covenant promises and covenant blessings. It is through the shed blood of Jesus Christ that the New Covenant was established. All the blessings and benefits of this covenant are yours when you believe in the Lord Jesus Christ and yield your life to Him.

The New Covenant is one of mercy and grace; cleansing and forgiveness; faith and hope; power and love; favor and son-ship. In the New Covenant, Christ is your righteousness, redemption, salvation, and sanctification. Through Him, the blessings of Jesus are poured out upon you; the glories of Jesus shine brightly around you; the beauty of Jesus is formed within you.

God's Presence

"You must always keep the special
Bread of the Presence on the table before Me."
Exodus 25:30 NLT

The bread that was used in the Tabernacle in the Old Testament was known as the "Bread of Presence." This bread actually referred to the "face of the Lord." The "Bread of Presence" was always on a table set before the Holy of Holies. In a very special way, the face of the Lord shines upon you as you partake of Him, the Bread of Life, and enjoy His tender presence.

Lord, I partake of You today. You are my life, my joy, my song. I breathe in Your peace, I abide in Your rest, I delight in Your nearness, I celebrate Your mercies, I embrace Your love with all my heart. Lord, I see Your face and I'm warmed by Your smile, I feel Your touch and I'm comforted by Your tenderness, I hear Your voice and I'm made to feel secure. As I walk with You today, my desire is to make Your heart glad.

Roy Lessin

Life

Jesus said to them, "I am the bread of life.
He who comes to Me shall never hunger."

John 6:35 NKJV

When Jesus spoke of Himself as the Bread, He associated it with life itself. Jesus' life is your life. He feeds you, nurtures you, and sustains you. You are totally dependent upon Him in all things and for all things that pertain to life and godliness.

Jesus, Your life is as sweet waters, Your touch is as healing streams, and Your joy is as bubbling fountains. Your beauty is more marvelous than a thousand sunsets, Your majesty is more awesome than the highest snow-capped mountains, and Your glory is more brilliant than the star-filled heavens. You are life and abundant life; You are grace and abounding grace; You are joy and fullness of joy; You are love and unfailing love.

Intimacy

"He who eats My flesh and drinks
My blood abides in Me, and I in him."
John 6:56 NKJV

Intimacy means to know someone at the deepest level. Through intimacy, you come to know the Lord heart-to-heart and spirit-to-spirit. Intimacy is at the very center of your love relationship with Him.

Jesus, I am Yours and Yours alone. You have no rival in my life. Your will has conquered my choices, Your kindness has conquered my doubts, Your mercies have conquered my will, Your grace has conquered my desires, Your goodness has conquered my thoughts, Your compassion has conquered my affections, and Your love has conquered my heart.

Roy Lessin

May

Love ... bears all things, believes all things,
hopes all things, endures all things. Love never fails.

1 Corinthians 13:7-8

Victory in Jesus

*Love ... bears all things, believes all things, hopes all
things, endures all things. Love never fails.*

1 Corinthians 13:7-8 NKJV

A mother once overheard her five-year-old daugh-
ter singing the popular hymn *Victory in Jesus*. The
little girl finished the hymn with this slight change
in the ending, "He loved me 'ere I knew Him, and
all my love is *through* Him."

When the mother heard the words "*through*
Him" something registered deep within her heart.
In her own words she shares the following:

All my love is *through* Him, who is the very essence of
love. This truth sets me free. I cannot love, but He can.
I cannot be patient, but He can. I cannot be kind ... I
cannot help but envy ... I cannot swallow my pride ... or
control my anger ... or forgive ... or trust again ... or keep
on giving ... but He can. Jesus can and does love others.
Through Him it is possible for me. And that is victory.

Unlimited Resources

*He commanded the multitudes to sit down
on the grass. And He took the five loaves and
the two fish, and looking up to heaven, He blessed
and broke and gave the loaves to the disciples;
and the disciples gave to the multitudes.*

Matthew 14:19 NKJV

As you look around, the needs that you see are often great and overwhelming. Your own resources seem so small, and your own abilities seem so limited to meet such great needs.

If you tried to quench the thirst of others out of your own fountain, no one would be satisfied; if you tried to feed the hungry with your own bread, no one would be made full; if you tried to reassure others with your own thoughts, no one would be comforted; if you tried to bring meaning to the lives of others with your own plans, no one would be fulfilled.

Jesus asks you to give all that you have to Him. As you place your life in His hands, He will break you as bread, multiply you, and use you to meet the needs of others with His unlimited resources.

Roy Lessin

Jesus Has No Limitations

Looking unto Jesus, the author and finisher of our faith.

Hebrews 12:2 NKJV

Jesus can meet the needs of an individual or a multitude because He has no limitations. He does not want you to set any limitations upon what He can do through you.

He is the only One who is able to quench the thirst of others with living water; who is able to fill the hungry with living bread; who is able to reassure the hurting with His comfort.

God has called you to look upon His Son and to point others to Him. It is His voice that others need to hear, it is His glory that others need to see, it is His will that others need to follow, it is His fullness that others need to receive, and it is His love that others need to embrace.

In God Alone

*Without faith it is impossible to please Him, for he
who comes to God must believe that He is, and that
He is a rewarder of those who diligently seek Him.*

Hebrews 11:6 NKJV

It is vital to your faith that you are able to see God as
all-powerful, all-sufficient, and all-mighty.

Your faith needs to bring you past the place of
saying, "God can do some things" to proclaiming,
"God can do all things." Your faith must move you
past the place of saying, "With God some things are
possible," to saying, "With God all things are possible."

Faith will never add the word "but" to any of
God's promises. Faith will never say, "God is my
provider, but if He doesn't come through I have
other options." Your faith must daily proclaim, "My
total trust is in God alone, my total dependency is
in God alone, and my total well-being is in God's
hands alone. I have no other options."

Roy Lessin

An Important Prayer

*[I am praying] that the God of our Lord Jesus Christ,
the Father of glory, may **give to you** the spirit
of wisdom and revelation in the knowledge of Him.*
Ephesians 1:17 NKJV

There are many things that you can pray about in a day. One of the most important prayers that should be on your lips is your desire to know God more and more. This is a prayer that God longs to answer. How does God answer that prayer?

Ephesians 1:17 tells us that God's answer does not come to us as information to our brain, but as revelation to our spirit. It is in your spirit that you come to know God in a personal and intimate way. Your natural mind can gather many facts and volumes of information about God, and yet not truly know Him at all.

In order for you to know God, He must reveal Himself to you.

The Holy Spirit, Our Helper

"Nevertheless I tell you the truth.
*It is to your advantage that I go away; for **if I***
do not go away, the Helper will not come
***to you;** but if I depart, I will send Him to you."*

John 16:7 NKJV

The Holy Spirit was sent, not to conceal the things of God from you, but to reveal them to you.

- He was sent, not to darken your understanding of God, but to enlighten it
- He was sent, not to mislead you, but to lead you into all truth
- He was sent, not to confuse you, but to lead you in the paths of righteousness
- He was sent, not to tell you all about others, but to tell you all about Jesus.

Roy Lessin

The Holy Spirit Was Sent

*"Nevertheless I tell you the truth.
It is to your advantage that I go away; for if I
do not go away, the Helper will not come
to you; but if I depart, **I will send Him to you**."*

John 16:7 NKJV

- The Holy Spirit was sent, not to misinform you, but to conform you to the image of the Son
- He was sent, not to frustrate you, but to comfort you
- He was sent, not to leave you guessing, but to show you things to come
- He was sent, not to pull you down, but to build you up
- He was sent, not to bring you partial joy or peace, but to fill you to overflowing.

His Footsteps, My Pathway

The Holy Spirit
Reveals God's Heart

*[I am praying] that the God of our Lord Jesus Christ,
the Father of glory, may give to you the spirit of
wisdom and **revelation in the knowledge of Him.***

Ephesians 1:17 NKJV

God doesn't ask you to guess what He is like, imagine what He is like, or try and figure out what He is like. God must reveal to you what He is like.

When God reveals Himself to you, it is as if He is lifting up a curtain that is blocking your view of Him. You don't have to passively sit back and wait for God to reveal Himself to you, or hope that He will reveal Himself someday if you continue to follow Him. The Bible encourages you to make your desire to know God a matter of earnest prayer.

As you pray, begin to listen to what the Holy Spirit is communicating to your spirit. The Holy Spirit is the only one who knows the heart of God, and He has been sent to reveal God's heart to you.

Roy Lessin

The Holy Spirit's Assignment

"He [the Holy Spirit] will glorify Me,
for He will take of what is Mine and declare it to you."

John 16:14 NKJV

It is important to listen to the voice of the Holy Spirit in your life, because He has so many good things to tell you.

The Holy Spirit has been given the assignment of telling you all about who Jesus is and all that He has received from His Father.

The Holy Spirit loves to talk to you about Jesus and magnify Him.

Mighty Weapons of Faith

"Let not your heart be troubled;
you believe in God, believe also in Me."

John 14:1 NKJV

The presence of a troubled heart is due to the absence of a believing heart. Faith is like a strong gate that keeps all unwanted visitors out of the fortress of our hearts, while keeping safely within, all the welcomed promises of God's kingdom.

Jesus never wants the visitor named "troubled" to gain any entrance into your life. "Troubled" wants to stir you up inside, like agitated water in a pool. "Troubled" wants to attack your emotions and keep you disturbed. "Troubled" uses weapons of fear, doubt, and perplexity. "Troubled" will try and harass you, annoy you, and defeat you.

But faith has mightier weapons! Faith's victory is in the stillness, the calm, the quiet, the rest, and the peace of Jesus Christ.

Roy Lessin

Forgiven and Free

What this means is that those who become Christians become new persons. They are not the same anymore, for the old life is gone. A new life has begun!

2 Corinthians 5:17 NLT

One of the ways that "troubled" tries to attack you is with condemning thoughts about your past. Instead of getting you to look up into the assuring eyes of Jesus, "troubled" wants you to focus on what you have done in the past.

Although you cannot change your past, you can be free from the condemnation of your past. This freedom comes through the blood of Jesus Christ.

In Christ, your past no longer has a claim upon you. Jesus does not hold the past over you, but washes it away. The blood of Jesus Christ speaks two powerful words over your past, "forgiven" and "free".

The Fruit of Repentance

"Therefore bear fruits worthy of repentance."
Matthew 3:8 NKJV

What does the subject of restitution have to do with the past? Restitution means that there may be some area in your past that the Holy Spirit leads you to make right. It may mean anything from restoring something that you've stolen, to apologizing for something you may have said or done.

This does not mean that restitution earns your forgiveness from the past. Restitution is always a testimony to others of the grace and goodness of God that has already taken place in your life. It is not about you trying to do something to earn forgiveness.

Restitution is not the same as your repentance, but it is the fruit of your repentance. Through it, others will be unexpectedly blessed and God will be glorified.

Roy Lessin

Your Place Is Prepared

*As it is written: "Eye has not seen, nor ear heard,
nor have entered into the heart of man the things
which God has prepared for those who love Him."*

1 Corinthians 2:9 NKJV

Another way that "troubled" tries to attack you is with condemning thoughts about your future. The attack may sound something like this, "There is no hope and no future for you. You have blown it too many times. What makes you think God will let you into heaven. You are not worthy enough or deserving enough to have what God has planned for those who love Him."

Jesus does not want you to be troubled about your future. The reason you are not to be troubled is that He has gone to prepare a place for you, and He will one day receive you and welcome you to the place that He has prepared.

In All the Will of God

Epaphras, who is one of you, a bondservant
of Christ, greets you, always laboring fervently
for you in prayers, that you may stand
perfect and complete in all the will of God.

Colossians 4:12 NKJV

There are three different dimensions to the will of God in your life:

The first is where you are,
the second is what you are doing,
and the third is what you are becoming.

God wants you to do what He has called you to do, in the place that He has led you, in a way that glorifies Him.

Roy Lessin

Demonstrate Your Love

I delight to do Your will, O my God,
and Your law is within my heart.

Psalm 40:8 NKJV

God wants you to be in His will in all areas of your life. His will happens in your life as a result of His Word being deeply planted in your heart.

When His Word is in your heart your feet will seek His pathway, your voice will speak His truth, your hands will do His work, and your life will demonstrate His Kingdom. His will and His Word are established in your heart because He has called you into a love relationship with Himself.

Because of that love relationship, His will is not a burden to you, but a delight; not heaviness, but a joy; not a task, but an opportunity for you to demonstrate the love that you have for Him.

Spiritual Growth

*We will hold to the truth in love, becoming
more and more in every way like Christ,
who is the head of His body, the church.*

Ephesians 4:15 NLT

Spiritual growth means that within the will of God,
you are walking in the light that you have. You are
saying "yes" to the things He is showing you, and
you are responding by faith.

Spiritual growth does not mean that you are perfect, it means that you are being perfected in your
walk with Him. Spiritual growth takes time and
God is patient with you. Spiritual growth means
that you are in the process of being conformed to the
image of Christ. Spiritual growth means that there
will always be new things to learn, new ground to
conquer, and new steps to be taken.

Spiritual growth means that you are daily seeking the height, the depth, the width, and the length
of God's love for you in Christ.

Roy Lessin

Walk in God's Will

Do not be conformed to this world, but be transformed by the renewing of your mind, that you may prove what is that good and acceptable and perfect will of God.

Romans 12:2 NKJV

Walking in the will of God is your daily calling. There is nothing higher, greater, or better that you can do. In order for you to walk in His will, you must be wholly committed to do His will.

Once you've settled that issue in your heart, then the wonderful blessings of God's will are wide open to you. The will of God for you is good, acceptable, and perfect in all that He has planned for you.

Live as Jesus Lived

*"For whoever does the will of God is
My brother and My sister and mother."*
Mark 3:35 NKJV

The will of God will always draw you close to the heart of Jesus, to the vision of Jesus, to the passion of Jesus, to the plans of Jesus, to the ministry of Jesus, to the words of Jesus, and to the ways of Jesus.

The will of God for your life will always bring you into a close and intimate relationship with Jesus, a sweet and tender walk with Jesus, and an enriching and enduring companionship with Jesus. To live in complete abandonment to the will of God for your life is to live as Jesus lived.

Doing the will of God means daily embracing the Father's will with all your heart, just as Jesus daily embraced the will of His Father with all of His heart.

Roy Lessin

Serve by Doing God's Will

For David, after he had served his own generation
by the will of God, fell asleep, was buried
with his fathers, and saw corruption.

Acts 13:36 NKJV

There can be no greater way to live your life than to serve your generation by doing the will of God. God has brought you into this world, at this time, for that very purpose.

God has a specific plan and purpose for your life that only He could create and only He can fulfill. When your life is yielded into His protective hands, nothing can defeat, destroy, or rob you of His will and plan. His will and calling on your life is a holy thing.

He will guard you, protect you, care for you, defend you, and keep you until you have fully finished the course and completed the race that He has set before you.

The Decision of Your Heart

As bondservants of Christ, doing
the will of God from the heart.

Ephesians 6:6 NKJV

If you seek to do the will of God based upon your emotions, then you will only do the will of God when you feel like it. If you seek to do the will of God based upon your reason, then you will only do the will of God when it sounds logical to you.

God wants you to do His will based upon the decision of your heart. He wants His will to be an outflow of your love relationship with Him. When you do the will of God from your heart, you are saying to Him, "Father, thank You for the privilege I have of knowing You and living for You. All that I do, is done out of my love debt to You."

Roy Lessin

Attitudes and Actions

*In everything give thanks; for this is
the will of God in Christ Jesus for you.*

1 Thessalonians 5:18 NKJV

The will of God is to be expressed in your attitudes as well as in your actions. If you do something that God has asked you to do, but do it with a grumbling or complaining attitude, you have not fully done the will of God.

Consider these powerful words that describe Jesus' attitude in going to the cross: "Looking unto Jesus the author and finisher of our faith; who for the joy that was set before Him endured the cross, despising the shame, and is set down at the right hand of the throne of God" (Heb. 12:2 KJV).

Clean Hands and a Pure Heart

For this is the will of God, your sanctification.
1 Thessalonians 4:3 NKJV

The will of God includes holiness and purity. Holiness is everything that is beautiful about God. His calling is a holy calling, His guidance is a holy guidance, His voice is a holy voice. His will for you is a holy will, His plans for you are holy plans, His purpose for you is a holy purpose.

His will for your life is that you have clean hands and a pure heart. His will for you is possible, not because you are holy, but because He is Holy and He lives His life in you.

His holiness is your holiness, His purity is your purity, His sanctification is your sanctification. The Bible declares, "But of Him you are in Christ Jesus, who became for us wisdom from God – and righteousness and sanctification" (1 Cor. 1:30 NKJV).

Roy Lessin

Reaching Others

God leads us from place to place in one perpetual victory parade. Through us, He brings knowledge of Christ.
2 Corinthians 2:14 MSG

The will of God is all about Jesus, what He did, what He is doing, and what He wants to do. And that involves you. Actually, you are His vessel, and He is the One doing the work, reaching others through you by His grace and mercy.

- His voice through you liberates others
- His touch through you heals others
- His acceptance through you restores others
- His compassion through you comforts others
- His grace through you encourages others
- His embrace through you assures others.

Patient Endurance

For you have need of endurance, so that after you have done the will of God, you may receive the promise.

Hebrews 10:36 NKJV

The will of God in your life is not just for the moment, but it is also for the long haul. There are some things that you will see God do instantly, there are other things that God will do progressively, and there are still other things that God will do eventually, in His time and in His way.

The important thing is not to set a timetable on God, or expect Him to do things the way you want them to be done. In trusting His will, you must also trust His wisdom and His timing.

God's waiting times are not meant to frustrate you, but to weave within your character, the qualities of patient endurance.

Roy Lessin

Doing Good Things

For this is the will of God, that by doing good you may put to silence the ignorance of foolish men.

1 Peter 2:15 NKJV

The will of God is in agreement with doing good things. You never need to feel bad about doing the will of God.

- God is good.
- God's laws are good.
- Jesus went about doing good.
- Everything that God made is good.
- God wants you to cling to what is good.
- God wants you to overcome evil with good.
- God wants you to trust in Him and do good.
- God wants you to be zealous about doing good.
- God works all things together in life for the good.
- God will not withhold anything from you that is good.
- God gives you the grace to abound to every work that is good.

Priceless Possessions

The world is passing away, and the lust of it;
but he who does the will of God abides forever.

1 John 2:17 NKJV

Jim Elliot, a missionary who was martyred in Ecuador, once made this powerful statement, "He is no fool who gives up what he cannot keep to gain what he cannot lose."

The things that are associated with this world – possessions, titles, fame, pleasures, wealth – are temporary and are passing away. The things that are associated with the will of God – goodness, righteousness, eternal life, peace, love – are part of the things that will last forever.

When people seek to hold on to the things of this world, it is like possessing a handful of sand that rapidly passes through their fingers. It is in doing the will of God that people will find the things that endure.

Roy Lessin

Doing Good – Regardless

For it is better, if it is the will of God,
to suffer for doing good than for doing evil.
1 Peter 3:17 NKJV

Doing the will of God is not always the easiest thing to do, but it is always the right thing to do, the highest thing to do, and the best thing to do. Doing His will may bring you discomfort, difficulty, persecution, rejection, suffering, or hardship. God never wants you to stop doing His will because there are those who oppose His will, reject His ways, and refuse to follow in His footsteps.

Jesus told us that we would have tribulation in the world, but to be of good cheer because He has overcome the world (John 16:33). Even though there were those who despised and rejected Jesus, He never stopped doing the will of His Father. He never stopped helping the helpless, loving the unlovely, and doing good to all.

Christ's Own House

Christ as a Son over His own house,
whose house we are if we hold fast the confidence
and the rejoicing of the hope firm to the end.

Hebrews 3:6 NKJV

Jesus is presented in Hebrews 3:1-6 in three ways: Apostle, High Priest, and Builder of His house (the body of Christ).

As Apostle, He lays the foundation of the house –
Jesus is the foundation of our faith.

As Builder, He constructs the house –
Jesus is building us together as living stones.

As High Priest, He attends to the affairs of the house –
Jesus is interceding and ministering to us in our development, so that we might be a bright, clean, well-furnished house fit for the Master's use.

Roy Lessin

Be Firm

Christ as a Son over His own house,
*whose house we are if we **hold fast the confidence***
and the rejoicing of the hope firm to the end.

Hebrews 3:6 NKJV

In the light of all that Jesus has done and is doing for you, He wants you to be firm in your response to Him.

He wants you to be firm in *confidence*, assured that He is doing the right thing, the good thing, and the best thing for you.

He wants you to be firm in *rejoicing*, thanking Him for what He is doing, and celebrating His skilled workmanship in you.

He wants you to be firm in *hope*, being certain that He will not abandon the work He has begun in you.

An Incredible Life

We know that there is only one God,
the Father, who created everything, and we exist
for Him. And there is only one Lord, Jesus Christ,
through whom God made everything and
through whom we have been given life.

1 Corinthians 8:6 NLT

You were made for God, and it is through the person of Jesus Christ that you have been given God's incredible life. What God desires, Jesus provides.

He is the entryway into the Father's companionship, He is the pathway into the Father's heart, and He is the doorway into the Father's royal chamber.

Roy Lessin

Only One God, Only One Lord

We know that there is only one God,
the Father, who created everything, and we exist
for Him. And there is only one Lord, Jesus Christ,
through whom God made everything and
through whom we have been given life.

1 Corinthians 8:6 NLT

Through the Holy Spirit, Jesus breathes the Father's breath into your spirit, pours the Father's love into your heart, and brings the Father's presence into your life.

Jesus is the bright light of the Father's glory, and He is the exact representation of the Father's person. Jesus is every word that the Father says to you, every thought that the Father has toward you, and every blessing that the Father gives to you.

June

Don't worry about anything; instead,
pray about everything. Tell God what you need,
and thank Him for all He has done.

Philippians 4:6 NLT

The Author of Originality

*"Behold, I will do a new thing, now it shall spring
forth; shall you not know it? I will even make a
road in the wilderness and rivers in the desert."*

Isaiah 43:19 NKJV

God is never outdated. He is never irrelevant. He is
not the God of "old ideas." God is eternally fresh,
always relevant, and continues to give newness of
life. God is the author of originality and creativity.

God is the God of new beginnings. He does new
things and is writing a new story in the life of each
one who trusts Him and walks before Him in faith
and obedience. God has something new for you
each day.

He may lead you down a new pathway, walk
you through a new door of opportunity, open up
a new insight into His Word, reveal a new aspect
of His Kingdom, bless you with a new relationship,
or send a new river of joy into a dry, desert place in
your life.

Eternal Plans for You

*I heard a great voice out of heaven saying,
"Behold, the tabernacle of God is with men, and He
will dwell with them, and they shall be His people,
and God Himself shall be with them, and be their God."*

Revelation 21:3 KJV

What "shall be" is where God "will be." The things that "shall be" give your faith many promises to look forward to in God's eternal plans for you in heaven.

- You shall be satisfied when you awake in His likeness (Ps. 17:15).
- Your inheritance shall be forever (Ps. 37:18).
- You shall be saved (Ps. 80:19).
- You shall be in the likeness of His resurrection (Rom. 6:5).
- You shall never be separated from His love (Rom. 8:39).
- You shall be changed (1 Cor. 15:52).
- You shall put on immortality (1 Cor. 15:54).
- You shall be with the Lord forever (1 Thess. 4:17).
- You shall be an heir of salvation (Heb. 1:14).
- You shall be like Him for you shall see Him as He is (1 John 3:2).

Roy Lessin

A Powerful Touch

*Then Jesus, moved with compassion,
stretched out His hand and touched him,
and said to him, "I am willing; be cleansed."*

Mark 1:41 NKJV

The touch of Jesus is a powerful thing in your life. His touch means that He has not pushed you away from His grace, His mercy, and His goodness.

His touch is a touch of compassion which extends His eternal love to you. His touch is a touch of healing that mends and restores everything that is broken. His touch is a touch of acceptance that brings you into His family and makes you holy and beloved. His touch is a freeing touch that releases you from all the guilt and condemnation of the past. His touch is a calming touch that calms all of your fears.

His touch is an empowering touch that strengthens you in your inner-man with courage and boldness to follow Him with all your heart.

Pray About Everything

Don't worry about anything; instead,
pray about everything. Tell God what you need,
and thank Him for all He has done.

Philippians 4:6 NLT

What a stress-releasing word of encouragement God has given to you as you journey with Him. God's invitation to prayer moves you beyond times of prayer, seasons of prayer, or moments of prayer. His invitation moves you into living in prayer.

Prayer is as the air you breathe and the atmosphere you live in. God never asks you to cut back your prayer because you are making too many demands upon His time and exhausting His energy. He invites you to pray about the biggest things in your life, the smallest things, and everything in between.

God welcomes every prayer you speak in your heart or utter with your voice. He wants you to pray about everything because He wants you to realize that He is in everything in your life.

Roy Lessin

A Prayer of Adoration

*"God is a Spirit: and they that worship Him
must worship Him in spirit and in truth."*

John 4:24 KJV

Lord, I worship You, for You are beyond the worth
of anything else I know or have. There is never a
moment in my life when I do not need You. Your
face is beautiful, Your love is wonderful, Your grace
is bountiful. Your ways are the highways that lift
me up to new vistas of Your greatness.

Your light outshines every star, Your splendor
dims every sun, Your glory transcends all that is
considered radiant. The cry of my heart is that You
would draw me closer to Your heart; take me deeper
into Your love; move me nearer to the place where
Your fullness is revealed. Keep me full, but hungry;
content, but needy; complete, but never satisfied.

The Goal of the Gospel

"This is eternal life, that they may know You, the only true God, and Jesus Christ whom You have sent."

John 17:3 NKJV

As wonderful as peace, joy, grace, mercy, forgiveness, and a thousand other blessings are to your spiritual life, they are not the goal of the gospel.

The goal of the gospel is to bring you into a loving, intimate relationship with the Giver of every blessing and gift. God wants you, above all things, to know Him. He wants your knowledge of Him to come out of your communion with Him. As your relationship with God grows in the depths of your spirit, you will begin to see as He sees, feel as He feels, care as He cares, think as He thinks, and love as He loves.

The more you know Him, the more your heart will long to please Him and make His heart glad.

Roy Lessin

To Taste God's Goodness

That I may know Him and the power
of His resurrection, and the fellowship of His
sufferings, being conformed to His death.

Philippians 3:10 NKJV

The heart that knows God, only wants to know Him more; to taste of His goodness only causes you to hunger for more; to drink of His pleasures only leaves you longing for more.

As you begin to explore God's ways, you discover that they are past finding out; as you begin to climb to new heights of His goodness, you discover that the tallest peaks appear as flatlands compared to the vistas that are beyond; as you begin to descend into the depths of His love, you discover an ocean that has no bottom or shoreline.

God is so great that He has given you all of eternity to know Him more, and more, and more.

Awesome in Splendor

"Who else among the gods is like You, O LORD?
Who is glorious in holiness like You – so awesome
in splendor, performing such wonders?"

Exodus 15:11 NLT

Although God is a spirit, the Scriptures use many human terms to help describe His greatness:

- His hands represent His power.
- His face represents His presence.
- His feet represent His authority.
- His fingers represent His creativity.

Roy Lessin

Awesome in Love

- His arm represents His salvation.
- His eyes represent His watch-care.
- His ears represent His attentiveness.
- His mouth represents His wisdom.
- His heart represents His love.

God is love. Whoever lives in love
lives in God, and God in him.
1 John 4:8

The Purpose of God's Commands

*Now the purpose of the commandment
is love from a pure heart, from a good
conscience, and from sincere faith.*

1 Timothy 1:5 NKJV

God's commands are not for the purpose of keeping you from something that is good, but for bringing you into all that is good. His commands are given so that your faith can grow strong and your heart can remain pure.

His commands do not deny you riches, but bring you riches that thieves can't steal and rust can never ruin. His commands do not place a heavy yoke of bondage around your neck so you cannot move, but His commands are like mighty pinchers that break loose the chains that had you bound.

The purpose of God's commands is to bring you into the flow of His love, the beauty of His holiness, and the countless joys of His presence.

Roy Lessin

God's Very Best for Your Life

One thing I have desired of the LORD, that will I seek:
That I may dwell in the house of the LORD
all the days of my life, to behold the beauty
of the LORD, and to inquire in His temple.

Psalm 27:4 NKJV

God's path for your life leads you into the paths of His glory, into the fullness of His joy, and into the endless pleasures of His presence. There is no reason for you to settle for anything less than God's fullness, His greatness, His abundance, and His very best for your life.

There is no need to gaze upon an empty field when you can look upon a hillside covered in wild flowers; there is no need to drink water from a muddy pond when you can dip your cup into an artesian spring; there is no need to eat breadcrumbs when you can feast at a king's banqueting table; there is no need to wear tattered rags when you can wear the robes of royalty.

There Is No One Like God

Great is the LORD, and greatly to be praised.
Psalm 48:1 KJV

God has no competition in heaven above or in the earth below. There is no one like Him, and there is no way that we can compare His greatness to anything that the world considers great.

God's greatness means that He is great in every way. He is exceedingly great. He is high and higher than any domain we know; He is mighty and mightier than any strength we know; He is strong and stronger than any power we know.

There is so much for us to behold about God's greatness that our devotion can be focused upon Him without any diversion; our gaze can be fastened upon Him without any deviation; our attention can be fixed upon Him without any distraction.

Roy Lessin

New Beginnings

The Lord said unto Joshua,
"This day have I rolled away the reproach
of Egypt from off you." Wherefore the name
of the place is called Gilgal unto this day.

Joshua 5:9 KJV

Gilgal is a place in the Bible that represents new beginnings. Gilgal was the first place the Jewish nation arrived at after they crossed the Jordan River under the leadership of Joshua.

It was at Gilgal that the covenant of circumcision was reinstated with the new generation of Jews that had been born in the wilderness. It was at Gilgal that the first Passover was celebrated in the Promised Land. Gilgal was the first fortified camp in the conquest of Canaan. There is a Gilgal for each believer in Christ.

Gilgal is your place of new beginnings – a place where the past is rolled away, a place where new steps are taken, a place where new areas in your life are conquered, and a place where new victories are won.

Bethel – God's House

*Jacob called the place
where God talked with him Bethel.*
Genesis 35:15

Bethel also represents an important aspect of your Christian journey. For every believer in Christ, there is not only a Gilgal, but a Bethel. Bethel means "God's house."

- Gilgal is your starting place; Bethel is your abiding place
- Gilgal is where you move forward; Bethel is where you fall to your knees
- Gilgal is where you trust God for the new things that are ahead; Bethel is where you remember the good things that He has done
- Gilgal is where you move out as a warrior; Bethel is where you bow down as a worshiper
- Gilgal is where you give God your strength; Bethel is where you give God your adoration
- Gilgal is where you renew your vision; Bethel is where you renew your passion.

Roy Lessin

Your Quick Response

While Peter thought on the vision, the Spirit said
unto him, "Behold, three men seek thee. Arise therefore,
and get thee down, and go with them,
doubting nothing: for I have sent them."

Acts 10:19-20 KJV

The voice of the Holy Spirit is perfectly aligned
with the will of the Father and the Son. His voice is
a clear voice, a peaceful voice, and a voice that will
always be in agreement with the Scriptures.

When the Holy Spirit has spoken clearly to you,
you must not debate it with your mind. Once this
occurs, your reasoning will quickly try to talk you
out of doing what God has asked you to do.

When the Holy Spirit speaks to your spirit and
directs you to do a certain thing, the best thing that
you can do is respond with a quick "yes," a cheerful
attitude, and prompt obedience.

Brotherly Love

Be kindly affectionate to one another with brotherly love, in honor giving preference to one another.

Romans 12:10 NKJV

God loves you personally and He loves the body of Christ collectively. He works with you as an individual, and He has placed you within the body of a great multitude of believers.

He never wants you to think of yourself as outside of the body of Christ. He has things for you to do and gifts that He wants you to express within the body of Christ. There are things that are unique to your calling and to the ministry that He has given you.

The gifts that He has placed within you are to help encourage, instruct, discipline, nurture, edify, and help prepare the body, the bride of Christ, for the coming of the bridegroom.

Roy Lessin

The Body of Christ

Throughout the New Testament we discover the ways that God wants the body of Christ to react to one another:

- "These things I command you, that you love one another" (John 15:17 NKJV).
- With all lowliness and gentleness, with longsuffering, bearing with one another in love (Eph. 4:2 NKJV).
- Be kind to one another, tenderhearted, forgiving one another, even as God in Christ forgave you (Eph. 4:32 NKJV).
- Let the word of Christ dwell in you richly in all wisdom, teaching and admonishing one another in psalms and hymns and spiritual songs (Col. 3:16 NKJV).
- No one has seen God at any time. If we love one another, God abides in us, and His love has been perfected in us (1 John 4:12 NKJV).

Be imitators of God, therefore,
as dearly loved children and live a life of love.

Ephesians 5:1

Made for God

*We know that there is only one God, the Father, who created everything, and **we exist for Him**. And there is only one Lord, Jesus Christ, through whom God made everything and through whom we have been given life.*

1 Corinthians 8:6 NLT

God the Father, God the Son, and God the Holy Spirit, are eternal. Everything else and everyone else has been created. The visible world and the invisible world are all made by God.

Every person, every plant, every animal, every star, and every spiritual being have been created by Him. There are many people who have been created by God that do not know why He created them. God wants you to know why He created you and placed you here.

God made you for Himself. Any other reason or explanation falls short of what God has in His heart for you, and diminishes your true worth and value to Him.

Roy Lessin

Your Highest Aim

Live a life filled with love for others, following
the example of Christ, who loved you and gave
Himself as a sacrifice to take away your sins.

Ephesians 5:2 NLT

Christ sets you free to pursue His love, walk in His
love, and express His love to others. Love, not freedom, should be your highest aim.

As you make decisions in life, the guiding question should not be, "Do I have the freedom to do
this?" but rather, "Is my decision the most loving
thing to do?" Decisions that are motivated by love
will move you closer to God's heart, strengthen
your faith, build up your spirit, enrich your life, and
encourage your heart.

Decisions made for love's sake will help you in
your spiritual growth, mature you in your spiritual
walk, and strengthen you in your spiritual development.

A Perfect Time for Everything

To everything there is a season,
a time for every purpose *under heaven.*

Ecclesiastes 3:1 NKJV

In your walk with God it is important to wait for God. As you wait, wait with a quiet heart, not a restless spirit. As long as your heart is set on God, you can be confident that everything that is in His will for your life will be yours in His time.

Someone once said, "With God, timing is more important than time." God didn't send His Son into the world at a random moment, but at the perfect time in history and at the perfect moment. If Jesus had come a generation sooner or a generation later He could not have been the promised Messiah, because He could not have fulfilled every prophecy that was spoken of Him.

God has a perfect time for everything that concerns you.

Roy Lessin

Seasons

*To **everything there is a season,***
a time for every purpose under heaven.
Ecclesiastes 3:1 NKJV

Within God's will for your life there will be seasons when certain opportunities, ministries, circumstances, and relationships move in or out of your life, like the seasons of the year that change around you.

There will be winter seasons when things are quiet, and you sense those special times when you are shut-in with God; there will be spring seasons when you sense renewal, freshness, and God bringing forth new vision and new direction in your life.

There will be summer seasons filled with growth, endurance, and strength for labor; there will be fall seasons when you will see beauty, change, and the ingathering of the harvest of your labors.

Living in the Light

For Thou wilt light my candle:
the L*ORD* *my God will enlighten my darkness.*

Psalm 18:28 KJV

When God lights up your life, He lights up your spirit with His glory. When you were outside of Christ you lived in spiritual darkness – God was a person you did not know, He had a voice that you did not hear, and He worked in ways you could not see.

Your spirit is like a candle in need of the flame of God's love. When God places His light within you everything changes – the voice of God becomes discernable, the ways of God become understandable, the presence of God becomes enjoyable, the will of God becomes desirable, and the fellowship of God becomes delightful.

The beauty of being in the light and living in the light of God is that you can live in unhindered communion with Him.

Roy Lessin

Christ's Ambassador

Now then we are ambassadors for Christ.

2 Corinthians 5:20 KJV

As Christ's ambassador you have a very special place and assignment in this world. Being Christ's ambassador means that you have not appointed yourself for service, but you have been personally appointed and sent by the King Himself.

An ambassador is someone who represents one kingdom within the realm of another kingdom. You represent the kingdom of God to the kingdoms of this world. As His ambassador, you stand under the complete covering and authority of the King and His Kingdom wherever He sends you.

A Prayer of Beginnings

*My voice shalt Thou hear in the
morning, O LORD; in the morning will I
direct my prayer unto Thee, and will look up.*

Psalm 5:3 KJV

Father, as I begin this day I commit it to You. I lay all things at Your feet. I place all things into Your hands. I move forward in faith, believing that You go before me. I receive from You – Your strength, Your enabling, and Your anointing. I embrace Your love, Your mercy, and Your grace.

Release through me, as rivers of living water, Your goodness, Your truth, and Your love. Take my heart and fill it, take my hands and use them, take my words and speak through them, take my feet and guide them. May Your glory be the signature over all I do this day.

Roy Lessin

The Holy Spirit of Promise

*In Him you also trusted, after you heard
the word of truth, the gospel of your salvation;
in whom also, having believed, you were
sealed with the Holy Spirit of promise.*

Ephesians 1:13 NKJV

There are so many wonderful names and characteristics of the Holy Spirit. In the book of Ephesians He is referred to as the Holy Spirit of promise. It means that the Holy Spirit's presence has been promised to you by God, and sent to you by Jesus.

"Promise" is such a soothing, healing, comforting word. The Holy Spirit of promise speaks with a voice of promise, and in a tone of promise. He does not come to you in tones of harshness, meanness, and cruelness. The Spirit of promise does not yell at you, scream at you, or threaten you. The Spirit of promise does not push you, drive you, or force you.

The Holy Spirit of promise assures you, prompts you, draws you, and woes you to the promises of God.

See the Perfect Day

The path of the just is like the shining sun,
that shines ever brighter unto the perfect day.

Proverbs 4:18 NKJV

One of the reasons you can become discouraged is when you don't see your life from God's perspective. God not only sees the big picture, but He also sees all the details of the picture. Your natural tendency is to look back and see your past failures, or to look at your present struggles and think that things won't change.

The way things are, are not the way things will always be. The important thing to realize about your future is that God is in it. He wants you to view your present situation in a greater light, with a deeper understanding, and with a steadfast assurance that He is always moving you forward into better things.

Roy Lessin

Complete Authority and Power

Jesus came and told His disciples, "I have been given complete authority in heaven and on earth."
Matthew 28:18 NLT

Too often we limit God because we look at our limitations instead of looking at His limitless power.

God never directs you to do what you think is best, but for you to follow what He knows is best; He never expects you to make a difference, but for you to allow Him to be the difference through you; He never asks you to trust in your resources, but for you to be dependent upon His.

Jesus said that He is the One who is in complete authority and has complete power.

Nothing Can Limit God

*He said, "The things which are
impossible with men are possible with God."*
Luke 18:27 KJV

Man is limited. There are only certain things that man can do, certain things that man can know, and certain things that man can discover.

God operates differently. God sees nothing as impossible, calls nothing impossible, and operates in a realm where all things are possible. God made every law that operates in the universe, and He can override any law that He has set in place if it pleases Him and is in accordance with His own will.

In the Scriptures we discover times when God changed the law of gravity, the laws of physics, the laws of biology, the laws of chemistry, and the laws of astronomy to perform His will. Nothing can limit the Lord.

Roy Lessin

God's Perfect Care

"With God all things are possible."
Matthew 19:26

There are no limits to what God can do for you. If God can forgive your sins, wash your heart clean, and save your soul, He can do anything that needs to be done to keep you and provide for you as you serve Him and do His will.

He kept the sun from moving in the sky in order to lengthen the time of daylight, He caused an axe-head to float upon the water, He turned regular drinking water into fine wine, He opened the eyes of a man born blind, and He fed a multitude of thousands with five loaves of bread and two fish.

This same God can take perfect care of you.

Follow the Footsteps of God

*He said, "The things which are
impossible with men are possible with God."*
Luke 18:27 KJV

Man can do many things as he operates within the laws that God has given him, but man cannot do the impossible, no matter how hard he tries or how long he labors.

It is a good thing for you to remember that as an ordinary person, with many weaknesses, flaws, and limitations, you can daily follow the footsteps of an extraordinary God, who alone can do the things which are impossible with men.

Roy Lessin

July

Rejoice in the Lord always.

Again I will say, rejoice!

Philippians 4:4 NKJV

What God Will, Can and Did Do

Read God's promises and you will discover what God *will* do:

> *I will praise You with music on the harp,*
> *because You are **faithful** to Your promises, O God.*
>
> Psalm 71:22 NLT

Pray and you will discover what God *can* do:

> *"Listen to Me! You can pray for anything,*
> *and if you believe, you will **have** it."*
>
> Mark 11:24 NLT

Count your blessings and you will discover what God *did* do:

> *Your righteousness, O God, is very high, You who*
> *have **done** great things; O God, who is like You?*
>
> Psalm 71:19 NKJV

Choose To Rejoice

Rejoice in the Lord always. Again I will say, rejoice!
Philippians 4:4 NKJV

In the story *Pollyanna*, the young heroine reminds the hard-edged pastor to consider all the "rejoicing texts" in the Bible. For the one who knows Jesus and is following His footsteps, there truly are a multitude of things to be glad about.

For a believer, gladness of heart is not based upon wishful thinking, fantasy, or pretending. Gladness of heart is a state of being, based upon the reality of who God is, what He is doing, what He has promised, and who you are in Him. Gladness of heart is also a choice that you can make, allowing your attitudes to line up with God's will.

It means that instead of grumpiness, you can choose cheerfulness; instead of gloom, you can choose celebration; instead of being disheartened, you can choose to rejoice.

Roy Lessin

Prayer Examples

Then He spoke a parable to them, that
men always ought to pray and not lose heart.
Luke 18:1 NKJV

When Jesus taught about prayer He said, "When you pray." He never said, "If you pray." There are special things that happen when you pray. Here are some examples from the Scriptures:

- When Hannah prayed for a child, she conceived and gave birth to Samuel, a gift that she gave back to God for His service (1 Sam. 1).
- When Elijah prayed, rain ceased to fall upon the earth. Three years later, when he prayed for rain, it returned to the earth (James 5).
- When Moses prayed for Israel regarding their rebellion, God held back His hand of judgment over them (Exod. 32).
- When Solomon prayed and asked God for a wise and discerning heart to rule His people, God gave him more wisdom than anyone had ever known (1 Kings 3).

Special Things
Happen While You Pray

Then He spoke a parable to them, that
men always ought to pray and not lose heart.

Luke 18:1 NKJV

There are special things that happen while you pray.
The Scriptures give you examples to encourage you
to pray and not to lose heart.

- While Daniel was praying, Gabriel was dis-
  patched by God to give Daniel understanding
  and revelation (Dan. 9).
- While believers were praying, an angel of God
  loosened Peter's chains and set him free from a
  heavily guarded prison cell (Acts 12).
- While Cornelius was praying, an angel stood
  before him and revealed that God would bring
  salvation to his house (Acts 10).
- While Peter was praying, he had a vision. This
  vision was used by God to send Peter to the
  Gentiles proclaiming the message of the Gospel
  (Acts 10).

Roy Lessin

God Is an Eternal Thinker

Known to God from eternity are all His works.
Acts 15:18 NKJV

God doesn't need to be a "quick thinker," because things don't take Him off-guard or catch Him by surprise. God is an eternal thinker. He plans according to what was, what is, and what will be. His Word is a revelation to us of what He has known from eternity.

The promise of the Savior was an eternal plan, the family line through which God's Son would come to earth was known from the beginning, the shedding of Christ's blood on the cross was provided by God before sin ever entered this world.

God, who has been working out His great plan of redemption in this present world, is also working out His personal plan for your life. You have been in His heart for a long, long time.

God's Eternal Plan

This is His plan: At the right time He will
bring everything together under the authority
of Christ — everything in heaven and on earth.

Ephesians 1:10 NLT

God's plan not only includes what has happened from the beginning until the present time, but it includes everything that will ever be. Where is everything heading? It has one destination. Everything is heading toward Jesus Christ. God's Son is the central figure in His eternal plan.

In God's perfect time, everything will come under the complete authority of Jesus Christ. It is Jesus who will have the final say in all matters. Keep your eyes on Jesus; keep your faith in Jesus; keep your walk with Jesus.

As you continue to allow His footsteps to be your pathway, you will be moving into the very heart of God's eternal plan. Up ahead, you will see His millennial rule and His eternal reign.

Roy Lessin

Free Citizen of Christ's Kingdom

*Stand fast therefore in the liberty wherewith
Christ hath made us free, and be not
entangled again with the yoke of bondage.*

Galatians 5:1 KJV

God is a bondage breaker. God does not want you to be under any law that is outside the law of love. Christ came to set you free from anything that is not in His will or plan for you.

Bondage is any weight that tries to slow you down, pull you down, or keep you down as you seek to walk upon God's pathway for your life. In Christ, you no longer need to be a slave to any sin, any fear, or any lie of the enemy. You are a free citizen of Christ's Kingdom and have a rightful claim to all its blessings, freedoms, and privileges. As someone who is free in Christ, there is nothing to prevent you from fully possessing and enjoying the life He has given you.

Spiritual Freedom

"For if ye forgive men their trespasses,
your heavenly Father will also forgive you."

Matthew 6:14 KJV

One weight that God does not want you to carry is the weight of unforgiveness.

It is an attitude of the heart that abides outside the law of love. To walk in forgiveness is to walk in great spiritual freedom. Your heart is light when it does not carry a grudge, bitterness, or resentment. To forgive does not mean that you agree with the offence that someone has committed, or that you support it in anyway.

To forgive means that you choose to release the judgment you are carrying toward someone, even though that person did something that was unkind or unfair. The choice to forgive is not based on fairness or justice, but on mercy and grace. Mercy triumphs over judgment when you choose to forgive.

Roy Lessin

Keep Your Eyes on God

"O our God, will You not judge them? For we
have no power against this great multitude that is
coming against us; but our eyes are upon You."

2 Chronicles 20:12 NKJV

In your own strength and in your own wisdom you
are vulnerable, but God never wants you to be in a
place where you are dependent upon yourself. God
never wants your confidence to rest upon your own
understanding.

- It is one thing to know that there is a great enemy against you; it is another thing to know that God is greater than any enemy you face.
- It is one thing to know that you are weak; it is another thing to know that God is all-powerful.
- It is one thing to know that you don't have the answers; it is another thing to know that God has perfect wisdom, knowledge and understanding.

You will never face defeat as long as your eyes
are upon, and your trust is in the One who knows
no defeat.

His Footsteps, My Pathway

Things That Your Heavenly Father Wants To Tell You

See how very much our heavenly Father loves us, for He allows us to be called His children, and we really are! But the people who belong to this world don't know God, so they don't understand that we are His children.

1 John 3:1 NLT

- I love you.
- I've saved you.
- You are My child.
- You belong to Me.
- I will take care of you.
- I will provide for your needs.
- I have called you and I support you.
- No one will be able to loosen My grip on you.
- I have adopted you and made you a part of My family.
- I am preparing a place for you and you will live with Me forever.

Roy Lessin

More Things That Your Heavenly Father Wants To Tell You

"Fear not, for I have redeemed you;
I have summoned you by name; you are Mine."
Isaiah 43:1

- I give you My rest.
- I give you My peace.
- I have totally accepted you.
- You are under My covering.
- My love for you is unconditional.
- I delight in knowing you are Mine.
- You are someone that I highly value.
- I will bless the lives of others through you.
- I want to have unbroken fellowship with you.
- I want you to know My heart and be assured of My favor.

Questions for
Your Heart To Answer

The hearts of the wise lead them to do right.

Ecclesiastes 10:2 NLT

- Are the things that are important to God, important to you?
- Are the things that God values, valuable to you?
- Are God's desires what you desire?
- Does it hurt you more to fail God than to have someone fail you?
- Is it more important for you to please God than to please others?
- What is it that God would have you do today that will let someone else know that He loves them?

Roy Lessin

Increase Your Capacity To Receive

*We have all benefited from the rich blessings He
brought to us – one gracious blessing after another.*

John 1:16 NLT

God does not need to increase His capacity to give
to you, but you need to increase your capacity to
receive from Him. God's resources are never de-
creased, diminished, or depleted. The blessings that
God sends to you are not measured out by allotment. God doesn't say, "Your blessing allotment for
this month is 100. Since I have already sent you 99
blessings this week, you only have 1 blessing left for
the entire month."

Your desire before the Lord should be that He
enlarge you, grow your faith, and make your vessel
deeper, taller, and wider so that you can move from
fullness to greater fullness, from fruit to much fruit,
and from streams of love to rivers of love.

A Prayer of Affirmation
(Based on Psalm 37:3-8)

Lord, my trust is in You. I respond to Your goodness by responding to others in ways that are good. I thank You that You have guided my feet to the place where I am now living. Your faithfulness is my daily portion. I delight in You and in the desires that You have placed within my heart.

My ways are committed to You, my plans are yielded to You, my future is dependent upon You. I know that You will not fail to fulfill Your promises in my life. I have no plans but Your plans, no goals but Your goals, no agenda but Your agenda. I rest in You, I wait for You, I long for You. Thank You, Lord, You are so good to me.

Roy Lessin

A Great Assurance

Behold, the LORD's hand is not
shortened, that it cannot save.

Isaiah 59:1 *NKJV*

Imagine a man being in a deep pit with no hope of
escape, when suddenly he hears a voice from above
saying, "Don't worry, I will drop you a rope." Hope
is restored, but when the rope is dropped into the
pit, the man discovers it is too short to reach him
and bring him up.

When you turn from your sin to God for salvation, how blessed you are to have the assurance that
you will not come up empty. One of the great assur-
ances you have of your salvation is that God's hand
is not too short to reach you; His heart is not too distant to care about you; His power is not too limited
to pull you out of your horrible pit of need.

Gain All that God Gives

Yet indeed I also count all things loss for the
excellence of the knowledge of Christ Jesus my Lord,
for whom I have suffered the loss of all things,
and count them as rubbish, that I may gain Christ.

Philippians 3:8 NKJV

A follower of Jesus Christ always gains more than he loses, receives more than he gives away, and inherits more than he has forsaken. To gain Christ is to gain all that God has to give.

What you have in the natural realm is as nothing compared to what you receive in the spiritual realm; what you know with your natural mind is as nothing compared to what you will gain in spiritual understanding; what you have achieved through human effort is as nothing compared to what Christ will do through you.

Your life now is not about your abilities, but about His gifting; not about your powers of persuasion, but about His anointing; not about your energy, but about His enabling.

Roy Lessin

A Life of Excellence

*Yet indeed I also count all things loss for the
excellence of the knowledge of Christ Jesus my Lord,
for whom I have suffered the loss of all things,
and count them as rubbish, that I may gain Christ.*

Philippians 3:8 NKJV

Your life in Christ is not about the facts your mind
has gathered, but about the revelation your spirit
has received; it's not about you being a nice person,
but about His character being formed in you; it's
not about you being clever, but about you having
the mind of Christ.

Your life is not about your influence, but about
His favor; it's not about you being noticed or recognized, but about His glory; it's not about what
you look like, but about His image being formed in
you. To live for Christ means that you have chosen a
life of excellence, of wholeness, of fullness, of completeness, and of magnificence, because in all things
Jesus Christ has the preeminence.

One Small Word

"Let us be glad and rejoice and give Him glory."
Revelation 19:7 NKJV

Throughout the Bible there are small words that make a powerful impact upon our lives. Consider the word "Let". To "let" means that we have a responsibility in a given matter. It means that we must give permission or allow the opportunity for God to do something in our lives, or through our lives, that He desires to see happen.

When God says, "Let," He is telling us that there is no reluctance on His part to see something happen, but that He is waiting upon us to respond.

Roy Lessin

Your "Let" Responsibilities

Some of the "Lets" we find in the Bible:

- Beloved, let us love one another, for love is of God; and everyone who loves is born of God and knows God (1 John 4:7 NKJV).
- My little children, let us not love in word or in tongue, but in deed and in truth (1 John 3:18 NKJV).
- Therefore let those who suffer according to the will of God commit their souls to Him in doing good, as to a faithful Creator (1 Pet. 4:19 NKJV).
- Yet if anyone suffers as a Christian, let him not be ashamed, but let him glorify God in this matter (1 Pet. 4:16 NKJV).
- If any of you lacks wisdom, let him ask of God, who gives to all liberally and without reproach, and it will be given to him. But let him ask in faith, with no doubting, for he who doubts is like a wave of the sea driven and tossed by the wind (James 1:5-6 NKJV).

Let us not become weary in doing good, for at the proper time we will reap a harvest if we do not give up.

Galatians 6:9

More Things To Allow

More of the "lets" we find in the Bible:

- If anyone speaks, let him speak as the oracles of God. If anyone ministers, let him do it as with the ability which God supplies (1 Pet. 4:11 NKJV).
- For "He who would love life and see good days, let him refrain his tongue from evil, and his lips from speaking deceit. Let him turn away from evil and do good; let him seek peace and pursue it" (1 Pet. 3:10-11 NKJV).
- Is anyone among you sick? Let him call for the elders of the church, and let them pray over him, anointing him with oil in the name of the Lord (James 5:14 NKJV).
- Is anyone among you suffering? Let him pray. Is anyone cheerful? Let him sing psalms (James 5:13 NKJV).
- "Let not your heart be troubled: ye believe in God, believe also in Me" (John 14:1 KJV).

If anyone is in Christ,
he is a new creation.
2 Corinthians 5:17

Roy Lessin

Things God Desires To See

More of the "lets" we find in the Bible:

- But above all, my brethren, do not swear, either by heaven or by earth or with any other oath. But let your "Yes," be "Yes," and your "No," "No," lest you fall into judgment (James 5:12 NKJV).
- Who is wise and understanding among you? Let him show by good conduct that his works are done in the meekness of wisdom (James 3:13 NKJV).
- So then, my beloved brethren, let every man be swift to hear, slow to speak, slow to wrath (James 1:19 NKJV).
- The Spirit and the bride say, "Come!" And let him who hears say, "Come!" And let him who thirsts come. Whoever desires, let him take the water of life freely (Rev. 22:17 NKJV).

Christ lives in me.
Galatians 2:20

Daily Victories

For every child of God defeats this evil
world by trusting Christ to give the victory.
1 John 5:4 NLT

As God's child, there are daily victories that Christ will give you as you trust in Him.

In a world that lives in bondage to sin, Christ gives you freedom from sin; in a world of disobedience to God and His Word, Christ works His meekness into your heart; in a world of unbelief, Christ takes you on from faith to faith; in a world that is under the power of the evil one, Christ sends the power of His Holy Spirit within you; in a world of misuse and abuse, Christ leads you into all that is good and right.

In a world that lives in worry and fear, Christ gives you His perfect peace; in a world that is selfish and self-centered, Christ fills you with His unconditional love.

Roy Lessin

Being Prosperous

Beloved, I wish above all things that thou mayest prosper and be in health, even as thy soul prospereth.

3 John 2 KJV

God wants you to prosper, and being prosperous is a good thing to pray for in your life and in the lives of others. Jesus lived a prosperous life, but He didn't live a life of luxury. A prosperous life from God's point of view focuses on you being fully equipped for what He has set you apart to do.

To prosper includes not lacking in any gift that you will need to minister to others, not lacking in any provision that you will need to bless others, and not lacking in any grace that you will need to work with others.

An Audience of One

Having then gifts differing according to
the grace that is given to us, let us use them:
if ministry, let us use it in our ministering.

Romans 12:6-7 NKJV

The word "ministry" means the act of serving. It is not a word that refers to something huge, splashy, popular, dynamic, or prestigious. A minister takes the lowly place, not the exalted place; he does not walk above others, but washes their feet; he does not labor for the applause of others, but for the "well done" of his Heavenly Father.

Having a ministry does not mean always being noticed, being at the top, or doing something on a grand-scale. A true minister does his work for an audience of One, for the approval of One, and for the love of One, whether that ministry touches few or many.

Roy Lessin

God Forgives,
Cleanses and Accepts

*The sacrifices of God are a broken spirit, a broken and
a contrite heart – these, O God, You will not despise.*
Psalm 51:17 NKJV

The term "sacrifice" is often associated with something that you give up in order to do God's will. There is a much deeper meaning to this word. Sacrifice goes right to the core of who you are.

More than anything else, God is concerned with you offering your spirit and your heart to Him. A spirit that is proud and a heart that is hard will never be acceptable to God. When your spirit is broken and you come before God with your pride in pieces, God receives you with great grace and mercy.

When your heart is contrite and you walk tenderly before Him, God assures you of His forgiveness, His cleansing, and His acceptance.

Obedience, Your Best Preparation

He saith unto them, "Follow Me,
and I will make you fishers of men."
Matthew 4:19 KJV

What are you doing now? Do you sense there might be a change? Do you wonder what God has for you next? If a change is coming, you can be certain of some very key things.

First, you can be certain that it is the right change, because God makes no mistakes. Second, you can be certain it will come at the perfect time, because God is never late. Third, you can be certain that it will be a good change, because God will always do what is best.

How do you prepare for change? Your obedience today is your best preparation for tomorrow.

Roy Lessin

The Ultimate Giver

"Freely you have received, freely give."
Matthew 10:8 NKJV

God is the ultimate giver. He is abundantly generous and exceedingly bountiful. He gives and gives again. His blessings can't be counted, His abundance can't be measured, His generosity can't be contained. He has given you the blessings of earth and the blessings of heaven.

Because you have received so much, you have so much that you can give. You can give a smile, because God has smiled upon you; you can give a hug, because God has embraced you; you can give acceptance, because God has accepted you; you can give hope, because God has given you an eternal hope; you can give compassion, because God has given you comfort; you can give kindness, because God has given you love.

Perfect Partners

Grace to you and peace from God
the Father and our Lord Jesus Christ.
Galatians 1:3 NKJV

Peace is not found when you get into perfect circumstances. Peace is found because Jesus Christ, the Prince of Peace, has gotten into you. Joy is the perfect partner to peace and is found in the same way as peace. Joy is never found in what you have or what you do, but in who you have living in you.

You will show me the path of life;
in Your presence is fullness of joy;
at Your right hand are pleasures forevermore.
Psalm 16:11 NKJV

Roy Lessin

Beginning To Grow

Till we all come to the unity of the faith and of the knowledge of the Son of God, to a perfect man, to the measure of the stature of the fullness of Christ.

Ephesians 4:13 NKJV

Receiving the gift of Jesus Christ, and being born again is the beginning of the Christian life. From that point on, each of us has a lot of growing to do.

It is a normal process that takes place within us, and God patiently provides all that we need to grow strong and be healthy. He gives us the sunshine of His grace, the rain of His Spirit, the nourishment of His Word, the discipline of His love, and the benefits of His daily care. Each believer may be at a different place in his or her spiritual growth, but the important thing is that each of us continues to grow.

Growth means that we are growing up in Christ, in our faith, in our knowledge of Him, in our reflection of Him, and in our love for Him.

Eternal Life in Christ

"Search the scriptures; for in them ye think ye have eternal life: and they are they which testify of Me."

John 5:39 KJV

In Christ you have eternal life. Eternal life is not about heaven, but about a person.

Jesus Christ is eternal life. Eternal life is not about time or place, but about a quality of life that is higher, richer, fuller, and better than any other kind of life.

Eternal life goes on forever and it begins when Christ comes to live within you.

Roy Lessin

The Most Joyous Life To Celebrate

The gift of God is eternal life in Christ Jesus our Lord.
Romans 6:23 NKJV

Eternal life is the:

- sweetest life to taste
- most beautiful life to gaze upon
- most valuable life to possess
- deepest life to explore
- most glorious life to reflect to others
- most satisfying life to experience
- most fulfilling life to live
- most secure life to lean upon, and
- the most joyous life to celebrate.

August

The L<small>ORD</small> is my shepherd;
I shall not want.

Psalm 23:1 KJV

The God of All Things

*Now when all things are made subject to Him,
then the Son Himself will also be subject to Him who
put all things under Him, that God may be all in all.*

1 Corinthians 15:28 NKJV

The God of "all things" will not miss "one thing"
that concerns you.

- God is greater than our heart, and knows all
  things (1 John 3:20 NKJV).
- You created all things, and by Your will they
  exist and were created (Rev. 4:11 NKJV).
- "Behold, I make all things new" (Rev. 21:5 NKJV).
- The LORD hath made all things for Himself (Prov.
  16:4 KJV).
- "He who built all things is God" (Heb. 3:4 NKJV).
- I will cry out to God Most High, to God who per-
  forms all things for me (Ps. 57:2 NKJV).

Jesus' Preeminence

He is the head of the body, the church:
who is the beginning, the firstborn from the dead;
that in all things He might have the preeminence.

Colossians 1:18 KJV

Once the eyes of your faith gaze upon Jesus, it is easy to see why He has the preeminence in all things and over all things.

There is no other birth like His, no other life like His, and no other love like His. No one has ever walked as He walked, served as He served, or gave as He gave. No one has ever spoken as He has spoken, claimed the things that He has claimed, and demonstrated the things that He has demonstrated.

No one has ever suffered as He suffered, forgave as He forgave, died as He died, lives as He now lives, or intercedes as He now intercedes. No one has ever had the authority that is His, the name that is His, or the glory that is His.

Roy Lessin

Every Spiritual Blessing in Christ

Blessed be the God and Father of our Lord Jesus Christ, who has blessed us with every spiritual blessing in the heavenly places in Christ.

Ephesians 1:3 NKJV

Give your heart to Jesus, for He has given His heart to you, and so much more – He has given you His life, His truth, His peace, His promises, His assurance, His salvation, His mercy, His forgiveness, His acceptance, His Kingdom, His blessings, His provisions, His wisdom, His care, His power.

God has given His strength, His joy, His grace, His mediation, His intercession, His sanctification, His kindness, His goodness, His victory, His wholeness, His holiness, His righteousness, His fellowship, His companionship, His light, His bread, His tenderness, His compassion and His love.

A Walk in the Spirit

If we live in the Spirit,
let us also walk in the Spirit.
Galatians 5:25 KJV

Your Christian life is about a walk in the Spirit, not about a speed race in the flesh. To walk in the Spirit means that there is a pace to keep, a way to follow, a direction to be moving toward, and an endurance of purpose that needs to be daily maintained.

As the Holy Spirit leads you, He does not want you to come to the end of each day exhausted or gasping for spiritual breath. To walk in the Spirit means that your daily life is not so much about "big events," as it is about a quiet pace, a steady progress, a consistent disposition, a pleasing manner, a gentle spirit, a quiet heart, and a steadfast love.

Roy Lessin

Perfect Provision

The LORD is my shepherd; I shall not want.

Psalm 23:1 KJV

Sheep are one of the most defenseless creatures on earth. They have no fangs, claws, or sharp teeth to protect them against an enemy. They don't have great speed to outrun an attacker, nor can they climb a tall tree to get out of the reach of a strong foe. The only thing a sheep has going for it is the presence of a shepherd. The shepherd is the sheep's perfect provision.

The shepherd not only defends the sheep, but he also stays with them, and provides for them. Another important thing about a shepherd is that he doesn't lead the sheep at a gallop. A shepherd does not ride a horse and expect the sheep to keep up, rather, he walks in front of the sheep at a pace they can handle.

How God Wants You To Be

Let us walk in the light of the LORD.
Isaiah 2:5 KJV

Modern transportation moves us across vast distances at great speeds. These methods of transportation get us to our destinations rapidly, but they all have one common flaw, they do not allow us to observe, with any detail, the things that we pass along the way.

Satan moves people along at such a hectic pace that everything seems to fly past them, leaving them in weariness and exhaustion. They find little opportunity to be quiet, to reflect, or to dwell upon the reason why they are here and how God wants them to be.

When you walk in the Spirit, you are moving at a pace that allows you to explore, enjoy, and observe with great detail, the beautiful ways of God with you and the wonderful things He is doing all around you and within you.

Roy Lessin

By Whom All Things Are

*For it was fitting for Him, for whom are
all things and by whom are all things.*

Hebrews 2:10 NKJV

God has called you
to live your life under the One
who is over all things,
to follow the One
who knows all things,
and to trust in the One
who can do all things.

His Footsteps, My Pathway

Precious Thoughts

*How precious are Your thoughts
about me, O God! They are innumerable!*
Psalm 139:17 NLT

Something you need to be thinking about, is how often God is thinking about you. He thinks about you all the time. You are always in His thoughts and on His heart. He has thought more loving thoughts about you than you could ever count.

If you could count every grain of sand, on every beach and in every desert, you would still fall short of all the thoughts that God has thought about you. What kind of thoughts does God have about you? They are thoughts of good, thoughts of love, and thoughts of hope.

His thoughts include His plans for you. They pertain to your welfare, your purpose, your daily care, and your future.

Roy Lessin

A Solid Foundation

*For we have become partakers of Christ if we hold
the beginning of our confidence steadfast to the end.*

Hebrews 3:14 NKJV

The word "steadfast" is an important part of your
spiritual journey. This word helps to define the condition of your heart as you travel God's pathway.

You cannot be steadfast in your walk if you are
uncertain about God or His ways. To be steadfast
means that each step you take, however small or
big, will be taken in confidence, dependency, and
certainty in who God is and what He has said.

As a believer and follower of Jesus Christ, your
walk can be steadfast, not because you are steady
and consistent, but because the foundation under
your feet will always remain solid, firm, sure, and
unshakeable. You can be steadfast in your faith and
your obedience because Jesus Christ's love for you
will never waver, and His promises to you will
never fail.

A Prayer of the Steadfast

"Lord, teach us to pray."
Luke 11:1

Lord, I thank You for Your faithfulness. I thank You for the certainty of Your ways, Your Kingdom, and Your Word. I thank You that I can count on You, lean on You, trust in You, abide in You, and walk with You. Thank You that You are the foundation of my footsteps, the light upon my way, the destination I seek after, and the hope I carry in my heart.

I purpose to follow You in cheerful obedience, in singleness of focus, and in steadfastness of heart. Empower me, by Your grace, to keep on keeping on to do Your will. I thank You, Lord, for the assurance that You will never change, never falter, never waver, and never turn Your love away from me.

Roy Lessin

Your Labor Is Not in Vain

Therefore, my beloved brethren, be steadfast, immovable,
always abounding in the work of the Lord,
knowing that your labor is not in vain in the Lord.

1 Corinthians 15:58 NKJV

God wants you to remain steadfast, immovable, and always abounding in His work.

To be "steadfast" means that you will never let up or lay back from what He directs you to do.

To be "immovable" means that you will not be knocked off course through unbelief or doubt.

To be "always abounding" means that you will not take a "break from work" due to disobedience.

God never ceases to encourage you to be faithful to His call upon your life. One of the great promises that He has made is to assure you that your obedience to Him is never wasted, never empty, never meaningless, and never without a divine purpose.

Guardian of Your Speech

Let no unwholesome word proceed
from your mouth, but only such a word as is good
for edification according to the need of the
moment, that it may give grace to those who hear.

Ephesians 4:29 NASB

As you walk with God, He is concerned about the words that come out of your mouth – the things that you share, confess, affirm, and speak into the lives of others. It is a good thing to ask the Holy Spirit to be a guardian of your speech. The Bible tells us that we should be more involved with listening than we are with speaking (James 1:19).

It is freeing to know that God doesn't ask you to speak all the time, talk about anything, and have an opinion about everything. God does, however, give you great encouragement to speak things that are good, things that build others up, things that are bathed in grace, and things that come from His heart directly to yours.

Roy Lessin

Speaking without Words

There are many ways that you can speak good things into the lives of others without ever saying a word.

You can speak with the "face" of approval,
with the "eyes" of understanding,
with the "ears" of alertness,
with the "smile" of delight,
with the "tone" of kindness,
with the "spirit" of compassion,
with the "heart" of love,
with the "hands" of mercy,
with the "embrace" of acceptance,
with the "handshake" of companionship,
with the "glance" of interest,
with the "tears" of comfort,
with the "nod" of affirmation, and
with the "touch" of tenderness.

*Let us not become weary
in doing good, for at the proper time we
will reap a harvest if we do not give up.*

Galatians 6:9

His Footsteps, My Pathway

God Always Answers

You do not have because you do not ask.

James 4:2 NKJV

There are steps on your part, that will release things on God's part. Answers from God come to those who pray, God opens doors to those who knock, God guides the way of those who seek His ways.

- God's bounty comes to those who give.
- God's increase comes to those who labor in His fields.
- God's blessings come to those who bless others.
- God's love flows into the hearts of those who continue to give His love away.
- God's joy fills the souls of those who live to make God happy.
- God's fruitfulness comes to those who continue to abide in Him.

Roy Lessin

You Are God's Responsibility

Then turning to His disciples, Jesus said, "So I tell you, don't worry about everyday life — whether you have enough food to eat or clothes to wear."

Luke 12:22 NLT

It is easy to worry about something that you own, or worry whenever you carry responsibility for someone. There is a reason why God has commanded you not to worry about your life. The very moment that you turned your life over to Him, He took over the management, the watch-care, and the ownership of your life.

God tells you not to worry, because you are His responsibility. You belong to Him. He is perfectly able and His provisions are totally adequate to take complete care of you. You do not need to worry today, because you are no longer your own responsibility. His call to you is "Do not worry, but seek My Kingdom first, and with all your heart."

The Condition of Your Heart

Watch over your heart with all diligence,
for from it flow the springs of life.

Proverbs 4:23 NASB

Each of us has one heart, but each person's heart may be in a different condition or state before God. God wants your heart to be right toward Him. He wants your heart to be in a healthy condition so that the river of His love will be able to daily flow through you.

To watch over your heart is like watching over a garden. Make sure you are planting good seeds, nurturing the seeds that are planted, and pulling out any weeds that may appear. A healthy heart is a repentant heart, a tender heart, a cheerful heart, a giving heart, a yielded heart, a trusting heart, a devoted heart, a receiving heart, a humble heart, a loyal heart, an obedient heart, a rejoicing heart, a believing heart, and a thankful heart.

Roy Lessin

The Lord's Hand

Thou hast a mighty arm: strong is
Thy hand, and high is Thy right hand.
Psalm 89:13 KJV

The "hand of the Lord" is a powerful reference to God's ministry in your life. The Bible speaks about God's right hand, because the right hand refers to the hand of power, might, and strength. Jesus sits at the right hand of God, which means that Jesus is at the place of power and authority.

The Bible also tells us that God's hand is able to save you, to rest upon you, to lead you, to uphold you, and to lift you. His hold upon you is powerful, and no one can take you out of His hand. His hand can touch you, heal you, bless you, and comfort you. His hand is extended to you, and He will meet your every need.

His Footsteps, My Pathway

Christ's Life in You

*Now you belong to Christ Jesus. Though you
once were far away from God, now you have been
brought near to Him because of the blood of Christ.*

Ephesians 2:13 NLT

The Bible speaks about three aspects of your life –
who you once were, who you have become, and
who you are becoming.

- Regarding who you once were, the Bible declares, "You were dead in trespasses and sins"
- Regarding who you are, the Bible declares, "God
  made you alive with Christ"
- Regarding who you are becoming, the Bible declares, "You are being conformed into the image
  of God's Son."

It's good to have it settled in your heart that you
are done with the way things used to be, and that
God has put your old life to death upon the cross.
It is also good for you to know that you are living a
new life – Christ's life in you – and that God is moving you ever deeper into His light and His love.

Roy Lessin

Adopted into God's Family

His unchanging plan has always been to adopt us into His own family by bringing us to Himself through Jesus Christ. And this gave Him great pleasure.

Ephesians 1:5 NLT

Thank God today that you are not an orphan. You are not alone, insecure, unwanted, and without an identity. God has adopted you into His family.

He adopted you because He wanted you to be a part of His very own family. You are adopted with all the rights and privileges that belong to a son who has come into his inheritance.

What a Father you have! You have His love, His attention, His presence, His acceptance, and His name. You possess what He owns. His riches are yours, His other children are your brothers and sisters, and His home is where you belong.

His Footsteps, My Pathway

God Chose You for a Reason

Paul, an apostle of Jesus Christ by the will of God.

Ephesians 1:1 NKJV

Paul was not an apostle because he thought it would be a good career path. He didn't appoint himself for the office of an apostle because he thought he was best qualified, or because of his family background and education. Paul was an apostle for only one reason, God chose him to be an apostle. Paul didn't get to vote.

When Paul first met Jesus on the road to Damascus, Paul asked two questions. The first question was, "Who are you, Lord?" The second question was, "What do you want me to do?" If Jesus had said to him, "I want you to scrub pots for My glory," that would have been enough for Paul. What has God chosen for you to do? Are you doing it with all your heart?

Roy Lessin

The Truth in Written Form

That from a child thou hast known the holy scriptures, which are able to make thee wise unto salvation through faith which is in Christ Jesus.

2 Timothy 3:15 KJV

The Bible is like no other book. It is a living book, a holy book, and a God breathed book. The Bible is the truth in written form. It is an instruction book, a guidebook, a training manual, and a love letter. It is the Book of God, the Word of Christ, and the Sword of the Spirit.

It is likened to seed, compared to a two-edged sword, and regarded as milk for babes and meat for men. When you read the Bible with a heart of faith you will find promises to receive; when you read the Bible with a desire to obey, you will find a glorious pathway set before you.

When you read the Bible with a longing to know its author, the Bible will bring you into the inner-chambers of God's heart.

All for the Good

So be truly glad! There is wonderful joy ahead,
even though it is necessary for you
to endure many trials for a while.

1 Peter 1:6 NLT

God never gives bad deals or bad breaks to His children. First of all, God is good, and there is nothing bad in His nature or character. Second of all, God's love for you is far too great to give you anything less than His best. Tests, trials, or difficulties are never an indication that God has forgotten you, abandoned you, or short-changed you in some way.

God will use difficulty in your life for the good. God's own Son went through great suffering, but Jesus embraced that suffering knowing of the joy that was before Him in His Father's eternal plan. As God's child, you can be certain that one thing God will never withhold from you, or take away from you, is His very best.

Roy Lessin

Deeper Understanding

*May the Lord bring you into an ever
deeper understanding of the love of God.*

2 Thessalonians 3:5 NLT

Oh, the joys that belong to those whose hearts continue to grow in the understanding of how deep God's love for them goes, how complete His care for them is, how vast His thoughts about them are, and how abundant His blessings upon them will continue to be.

His Footsteps, My Pathway

An Unexpected Visitor

The church is His body; it is filled by Christ,
who fills everything everywhere with His presence.
Ephesians 1:23 NLT

Jesus will visit you many times in a week through the hands, the hearts, and the lives of His people, the body of Christ. You may not always be aware when He visits, but you can be certain that He does.

It may have been His voice that you heard in your last phone conversation; His touch that you felt the last time someone placed their hand upon you; His compassion you sensed when someone carried a burden for you in prayer; His warmth you recognized the last time someone greeted you with a special smile; His comfort that you received the last time someone gave you an encouraging word; His love you felt when someone did something for you that was quite unexpected.

Roy Lessin

Unforeseen Comfort

Whom I have sent to you ... that
He may comfort your hearts.

Ephesians 6:22 NKJV

Jesus will come to you
at the most unexpected times,
in the most unexpected ways,
and through the most unexpected people.

His Footsteps, My Pathway

In Christ You Have Everything

In Him (Christ) *you have been made complete,
and He is the head over all rule and authority.*

Colossians 2:10 NASB

Jesus Christ is above everything, before everything,
and ahead of everything in your life, in this world,
and in this universe. Before you ever sinned, He was
already your redeemer, waiting for you to come to
Him. When you had your first revelation of God, it
was Christ's image that you beheld.

Christ is your hope of the resurrection. Because
He has already experienced it, He has made it possible for you to experience as well.

Roy Lessin

Complete in Christ

*In Him (Christ) you have been **made complete**,*
and He is the head over all rule and authority.

Colossians 2:10 NASB

Are you empty?
  Christ is your fullness.

Are you weak?
  He is your strength.

Are you needy?
  He is your supply.

Are you confused?
  He is your wisdom.

Are you seeking?
  He is your destination.

Are you anxious?
  He is your peace.

Are you alone?
  He is your companion.

His Footsteps, My Pathway

Stand in Awe

To me, the very least of all saints, this grace was given,
to preach to the Gentiles the unfathomable riches of
Christ.

Ephesians 3:8 NASB

When it comes to the things of God and of Jesus Christ, we are always left in wonder, in amazement, and in awe. God can be called "The God past finding out", "The God of the so much more" or "The God beyond all measure."

Think of it, in a world where things are measurable, there is no way that we can measure God. We can't measure His love, it's too deep; we can't measure His goodness, it's too high; we can't measure His glory, it's too brilliant; we can't measure His grace, it's too abundant; we can't measure His blessings, they are too bountiful; we can't measure His strength, it's too mighty; we can't measure His mercy, it's too overwhelming.

Roy Lessin

The Perfect Path for Your Life

*"Yours is the kingdom and the power
and the glory forever. Amen."*
Matthew 6:13 NKJV

Why has God placed your feet upon the pathway that you are now walking? Why has He sent others on pathways that appear to be brighter, easier, or more glamorous than yours? The truth is, God has you on the perfect path for your life. There is a God-ordained purpose for each step you take. His purpose is to lead your life on a course that will most glorify Him. Here is a prayer that you can bring to God whenever you wonder what it is that He would have you do.

Father, please show me, as I walk with You today, what words I should speak, what choices I should make, and what attitudes I should carry that will most please You and make Your heart glad. Amen.

Carry the Cross God Gives You

Then He said to them all, "If anyone desires
to come after Me, let him deny himself,
*and **take up his cross daily,** and follow Me."*
Luke 9:23 NKJV

God does not want you to carry anything that He has not asked you to carry. Everything that He has asked you to carry, He will give you the grace to carry.

If you try to carry something that God wants someone else to carry, they will be given the grace to carry it, but you will not. If God has not asked you to carry something, do not pick it up.

God has called you to carry your own cross. His cross for you is something that you can take up daily, because grace will be in your hands to lift the cross, grace will be on your shoulders to carry the cross, and grace will be in your heart to live out the cross in your daily life. It is grace that makes bearing your cross possible.

Roy Lessin

Follow Christ

Then He said to them all, "If anyone desires
to come after Me, let him deny himself,
*and take up his cross daily, and **follow Me**."*
Luke 9:23 NKJV

Although taking up your cross involves denying
yourself, the main focus is about following Christ.
The cross you carry has to do with the choices you
make with your will, the responses you have in your
actions, and the attitudes you carry in your heart.

Your cross means that you are putting to death
every decision, every response, and every attitude
in your life that is not consistent with the love of
Jesus Christ.

September

My soul, wait silently for God alone,
for my expectation is from Him.

Psalm 62:5 NKJV

Wait on God

My soul, wait silently for God alone,
for my expectation is from Him.

Psalm 62:5 NKJV

To walk with God also means to wait on God. You may need to wait on God to fulfill a promise He has given you.

Joseph learned what it meant to wait for God to fulfill His promise to him. Joseph waited when his brothers sold him into slavery, he waited when he was a servant in the house of an Egyptian, and he waited when he was unjustly put in prison.

While Joseph waited he never threw away the promise, and while he waited, God worked. In God's time, the day came when He fulfilled every detail of the promise He had given to Joseph. Are you waiting on God? Be patient; be faithful; be true. Place all your expectations in Him; it will be worth the wait.

Undisturbed Peace

Let the peace of God rule in your hearts.

Colossians 3:15 NKJV

Peace should be the normal state of your walk with God. When you are out of God's peace, your walk with Him becomes troubled and an inner alarm goes off in your spirit.

When an umpire in a baseball game calls "Time out," everything on the playing field stops. The action is put on hold until the umpire once again calls "Play ball."

The peace of God abiding in your spirit is God's way of letting you know that all is well. When His peace is disturbed within you, it is time to stop and listen to what is causing the disturbance. The best thing you can do is to listen, obey, and get back into His peace as quickly as possible.

Roy Lessin

Living a Life of Love

And so, as those who have been chosen of God,
*holy and beloved, **put on a heart of compassion,***
kindness, humility, gentleness and patience.

Colossians 3:12 NASB

God has called you to live a life of love by coming into a love relationship with Him. This life of love is made possible because of the depth of God's love for you.

Living a life of love gives you the opportunity to demonstrate to others how much you are loved by God. The affirmation of God's love for you, gives you the confidence that is needed to demonstrate His love to others. You cannot freely love others if you question God's love for you.

One of the most powerful reasons why Jesus came and died on the cross was to settle forever, any doubt about the depth of the Father's love for you.

In God's Love

*And so, as those who have been **chosen of God**,*
holy and beloved, put on a heart of compassion,
kindness, humility, gentleness and patience.

Colossians 3:12 NASB

- In His love, God reached out to you; He did not ignore you or reject you.
- In His love, God received you; He did not push you aside.
- In His love, God embraced you; He did not turn His back on you.
- In His love, God cleansed you; He did not leave you in a state of uncleanness.
- In His love, God declared you blameless; He did not leave a weight of judgment hanging over you.
- In His love, God has called you His beloved; He has never turned His heart away from you.

Roy Lessin

You Are God's Beloved

And so, as those who have been chosen of God,
*holy and **beloved**, put on a heart of compassion,*
kindness, humility, gentleness and patience.

Colossians 3:12 NASB

You are God's beloved. To be God's beloved means that you are dear to His heart, that you are esteemed, and that He finds joy in you. He will never neglect you or disregard you. He loves you strongly, greatly, abundantly, and intimately.

To be God's beloved means that He will always be faithful to you, always want the best for you, and will always be good to you. As His beloved, He will pour favor, blessings, and benefits upon you. Knowing that you are God's beloved leaves your heart fulfilled, overjoyed, and eternally grateful.

Seated with Christ

*If then you were raised with Christ, seek
those things which are above, where Christ is,
sitting at the right hand of God.*

Colossians 3:1 NKJV

The heart of God is always moving you outward to
the needs of others, forward in your walk with Him,
and upward to your place in Jesus Christ. God has
seated you with Christ so that you can see life from
His point of view, value the things that He values,
and celebrate the things that He celebrates.

Because you are seated with Christ, you will
find that while your eyes have a forward look, your
heart has a heavenly focus; while your feet take you
on your earthly journey, your heart is pursuing a
heavenly direction; while your thoughts are busy
with temporal things, your mind is seeking the
things that are above.

Roy Lessin

Unconditional Love

We love Him because He first loved us.

1 John 4:19 NKJV

Our responses to others should not be based upon how we feel about them personally or how they respond to us. If we live that way, we will only be nice to those we like, or kind to those who are kind to us. If God only responded lovingly to those who first loved Him, we would be lost and without hope in the world.

Thankfully, God loved us before we loved Him. God loves us unconditionally, and it is His love that releases us to respond to others in a way that pleases Him. God never tells us to pick and choose the ones we will love, but He commands us to love others with the same love that He extends toward us.

Because of God, You Can

"Live generously and graciously toward others, the way God lives toward you."

Matthew 5:48 MSG

Because God loves you unconditionally, His love releases you to love others and do all He has commanded you to do.

- Because He has completely forgiven you, you are free to forgive others
- Because He blesses you, you are enabled to be a blessing to others
- Because God is good to you, you can do good to others
- Because He is merciful to you, you can extend mercy to others
- Because God is your Helper, you can reach out your hand to lift up others
- Because God bountifully extends His grace to you, you can be gracious to others
- Because God increases you, you can be generous to others
- Because God cares for you, you can extend compassion to others.

Roy Lessin

Words of Grace

*Let your speech always be with grace, seasoned,
as it were, with salt, so that you may
know how you should respond to each person.*

Colossians 4:6 NASB

Wrong words and unkind speech are like bitter herbs that season our speech. God wants our speech to be a beautiful thing that brings pleasing sounds to His ears, and imparts words of encouragement and hope to those who hear us. God wants our words to be "grace words."

- Grace words are words that influence the heart for good and are a benefit to the hearer.
- Grace words are words of favor and acceptance that extend a garment of kindness around the one who is being spoken to.
- Grace words carry a gentle tone and speak in understanding ways.
- Grace words include comments such as, "I will be praying for you," "Thank you so much," "Let me help you," "God bless you," "I understand," "I am sorry."

A Prayer for Opportunity

Meanwhile praying also for us, that
God would open to us a door for the word.

Colossians 4:3 NKJV

Father, order my steps, guide my way, and direct me to Your appointments and Your opportunities for this day. Make my way a prepared way, make my words wise words, make my responses loving responses. I ask that You would open the doors that need to be opened.

May those I speak to have open hearts to receive the words that Your Holy Spirit gives me to say. May they be timely words, spoken in due season, to meet the needs of those who hear. I pray for opportunities that will allow me to speak Your truth, Your light, and Your wisdom with clarity and unction.

Give me favor where favor is needed, grace where grace is needed, and boldness where boldness is needed to declare Your great love to needy hearts.

Roy Lessin

Listen, and Then Obey

*Abraham **listened** to Me and obeyed.*

Genesis 26:5 NLT

One important spiritual principle that we can learn from Abraham's walk with God is that *listening must precede our obedience* to God.

Sometimes a child can become so preoccupied with his toys that he will tune out the voice of his mother as she calls out to him. When God called out to Abraham, he did not tune God out. Abraham gave God his full attention, and as a result, Abraham knew what God wanted him to do.

Too often, God's children are not sure what God's will is for them because they are preoccupied with other things. It is important for each of us to keep our hearts quiet and attentive to what God is saying so that we will know what it is He wants us to do.

Obedience Precedes Revelation

*Abraham listened to Me and **obeyed**.*

Genesis 26:5 NLT

Another important principle we can learn from Abraham's life is that *obedience to God precedes future revelation from God*. When God told Abraham to leave his homeland, Abraham did not know where God was leading him. The revelation of the Promised Land came after he obeyed.

In another incident, God told Abraham to offer up his son Isaac on Mount Moriah. Abraham fully obeyed God's command. As Abraham was about to offer up Isaac, God stopped him and gave Abraham a glorious revelation of His redemptive plan, a ram caught in the thicket.

This ram would provide the sacrifice, and die a substitutionary death for Abraham's son. This revelation also points the way to the substitutionary death of the Lamb of God who gave His life upon the cross so we might live.

Roy Lessin

Overwhelming Generosity

"Is anyone thirsty? Come and drink –
even if you have no money! Come, take
your choice of wine or milk – it's all free!"

Isaiah 55:1 NLT

God is so overwhelmingly generous to you. He gives to you, and gives again; He blesses you, and blesses you again; He fills you up, and fills you again. God knows only one way to give, and that is abundantly.

God doesn't have class "A," class "B," and class "C" blessings. He gives only one grade of blessings – the best, the richest, the fullest, and the most valued. How can you receive these priceless blessings? You simply need to come and receive what He wants to give you.

Are you thirsty for more of Him? Come and drink. Are you hungry for what is real and true? Come and partake. Do you want to go deeper in your love relationship with Him? Come and hear His heartbeat.

His Footsteps, My Pathway

God Keeps You in the Light

*But **you aren't in the dark** about these things,*
dear brothers and sisters, and you won't be surprised
when the day of the Lord comes like a thief.

1 Thessalonians 5:4 NLT

In God's family, you are an insider, not an outsider. You are included in what is going on in Christ's body and in God's kingdom. God doesn't keep you in the darkness; He keeps you in the light.

This does not mean that you know everything that God is doing, but it does mean that God will give you all the light and understanding that you need to do His will and be prepared for what He has planned for you.

Roy Lessin

Live in Readiness Daily

*But you aren't in the dark about these things,
dear brothers and sisters, and **you won't be surprised
when the day of the Lord comes** like a thief.*

1 Thessalonians 5:4 NLT

How can you be ready for Christ's return? You will be ready because God will prepare you and make you ready. Even though you don't know the exact time when Christ will return, it doesn't mean that His return has to take you by surprise.

To be ready is to daily live in readiness. Simply walk in the light that you have been given. Do what you know to do, follow what you know to follow, and believe what you know to believe based upon what God has shown you in His Word and revealed to you by His Holy Spirit. He will not leave you behind.

The Right Step

*"Who then is the faithful and sensible slave whom
his master put in charge of his household to give them
their food at the proper time? Blessed is that slave
whom his master finds so doing when he comes."*

Matthew 24:45-46 NASB

Whether you are living in hard-times or in the end-times, God wants you to continue following the assignment that He has given you. A step of obedience is always the right step to take.

Faithfully stick to the task, faithfully follow His leading, and faithfully stay on the course that has been set before you. God does not want His children to pack-it-in, to back off, to retreat, to close-up shop, or to throw up frustrated hands and say, "What's the use!"

Do you sense His return drawing closer? Roll up your sleeves and keep on working. Do you sense the world growing darker? Trim your wick and let your light shine even brighter. Do you sense great needs all around you? Let the flow of His love continue to be poured out through your life as a healing fountain.

Roy Lessin

Live in Anticipation

"Be dressed for service and well prepared, as though you were waiting for your master to return from the wedding feast. Then you will be ready to open the door and let him in the moment he arrives and knocks.

Luke 12:35

Here are some instructions from Jesus regarding how He wants you to live as you await His return:

- Do not be deceived
- Do not be troubled
- Proclaim the gospel
- Endure to the end
- Be watchful
- Be prayerful
- Be faithful
- Be awake
- Be ready.

From Matthew 24 and Mark 13

Jesus Is Coming!

*You are looking forward to the coming of God's
Son from heaven – Jesus, whom God raised
from the dead. He is the one who has rescued
us from the terrors of the coming judgment.*

1 Thessalonians 1:10 NLT

As a believer in Jesus Christ you have so much to look forward to as you wait for God to fulfill His eternal plan, and send His Son from heaven. How blessed you are to be able to anticipate that day instead of dread it; to plan for that day instead of ignore it; to celebrate that day instead of fear it.

The perfect love that Jesus demonstrated for you when He died upon the cross is the same love that frees you from the fear of the judgment that is to come. Jesus is not coming as your enemy, or your foe. Jesus is coming as your Savior, your Bridegroom, your King, your Redeemer, and your Lord.

Roy Lessin

Jesus Reigns

He shall reign for ever and ever.
Revelation 11:15 KJV

Jesus reigns. He reigns in life, He reigns in death, He reigns in the heavens, and He reigns overall. He reigns above kingdoms and He reigns above kings. He reigns above darkness, every demon of hell, and He reigns above every circumstance of life.

He reigns above every sorrow of the heart, every need of the body, every choice of the will, and every emotion of the soul. He reigns with all authority, He reigns with all justice, He reigns with all righteousness, He reigns with all goodness, and He reigns with all might.

He reigns over the plans of men and the schemes of the devil, He reigns over the laws of the universe and the laws of nature, He reigns over the earth, the climate, the storms at sea, and of His reign and of His kingdom there will be no end.

Amazing Joy, Amazing Grace

*And you became followers of us and of
the Lord, having received the word in much
affliction, with joy of the Holy Spirit.*

1 Thessalonians 1:6 NKJV

As you faithfully follow the Lord you will experience affliction from those who oppose the Lord. Affliction is a very real part of every believer's journey here on earth. Affliction includes anything that brings difficulty, tribulation, persecution, or trouble because of your love for Jesus Christ.

The Bible tells us that the early believers celebrated when they were persecuted for their faith. That response is possible because there is an amazing grace that God gives to you when you walk through afflictions of any kind.

It is a grace that provides you with an inner joy even during the hardest of times. This joy is produced by the Holy Spirit. It is the Holy Spirit who puts within you everything you need to endure.

Roy Lessin

Blessings for Now – and Later

If we endure hardship, we will reign with Him.

2 Timothy 2:12 NLT

There are many blessings that belong to those who endure hardship. Some of those blessings are for now and others are for later. The grace and joy that are yours in the Holy Spirit are an important part of your present blessings. As wonderful and precious as these blessings are, the future blessings are quite astonishing.

As you continue to serve the One who reigns over all, you will one day join Him and reign with Him when He returns to establish His kingdom here on earth. Think of it, you will actually reign with the One who now reigns over you!

What a glorious future is ahead of you. No wonder the Bible declares, "What we suffer now is nothing compared to the glory He will give us later" (Rom. 8:18 NLT).

Look To God

And for this reason we also constantly thank God
that when you received from us the word of
God's message, you accepted it not as the word
of men, but for what it really is, the word of God,
which also performs its work in you who believe.

1 Thessalonians 2:13 NASB

Many people search for life's answers by looking within. The Bible does not tell us to look within ourselves, but rather to look to God, who works within us the things that are pleasing in His sight.

From the day you were born again of the Holy Spirit, a great work of God began within you. The Bible declares that Christ lives in you, and if Christ lives in you, the kingdom of God is within you. Because Christ lives in you, His Word is also alive in you.

Wherever Jesus goes His Word goes, and wherever His Word goes, change takes place. His Word will perform a mighty work within you, bringing truth, light, and wisdom; purity, holiness, and righteousness; nourishment, encouragement, and fruitfulness.

Roy Lessin

God Wants What's Best

*Beware lest anyone cheat you through
philosophy and empty deceit, according to the
tradition of men, according to the basic principles
of the world, and not according to Christ.*

Colossians 2:8 NKJV

- The world wants to improve people; God wants to transform people
- The world seeks to change people from the outside in; God seeks to change people from the inside out
- The world starts with the mind; God starts with the spirit
- The world works through reason; God works through faith
- The world declares philosophy; God declares truth
- The world points to man, God points to Jesus.

An Upside-Down Life

*For I am the least of all the apostles, and
I am not worthy to be called an apostle after
the way I persecuted the church of God.*

1 Corinthians 15:9 NLT

When you look at your life and compare it to God's life, it becomes quite overwhelming to realize that you are a recipient of His love. When you compare your sins, your failures, and your defeats with His holiness, goodness, and righteousness, it can prompt you to ask, "Who am I that God should be kind and generous toward me?"

As hard as it may be to fully understand, the fact remains that the Creator of all things, the omnipotent God, has sent His Son, Jesus Christ, into your life. Yes, "little you" is a recipient of Almighty God's all-encompassing, all-embracing goodness, kindness and generosity in Jesus Christ.

God, in His mercy and grace, delights in giving the highest to the lowliest, the greatest to the smallest, the fullest to the emptiest, and the mightiest to the weakest.

Roy Lessin

With You for Eternity

For the Lord your God is merciful –
He will not abandon you or destroy you
or forget the solemn covenant He made.

Deuteronomy 4:31 NLT

The God who formed you at birth, the God who gave you breath, the God who loves you every moment of every day, the God who has sent His Son to save you and claim you as His own, the God who is your dear heavenly Father, the God who cares for you, the God who is for you ...

Is the God who will never abandon you in life, harm you in death, or forsake you throughout eternity.

Jesus Prays for You

"Neither pray I for these alone, but for them also which shall believe on Me through their word."
John 17:20 KJV

You can always be rich in the things of God and in your walk with Him because of Jesus' prayers for you. Jesus began praying for you two thousand years ago. You were included in Jesus' high priestly prayer that He brought before His Father when His time and ministry on earth was about to end.

Through Jesus' intercession on your behalf, the riches of heaven have been opened to you, the blessings of heaven have been released to you, the realities of heaven have been given to you, and the resources of heaven have been committed to you.

Roy Lessin

Pleasing God Alone

"I have glorified You on the earth. I have finished the work which You have given Me to do."
John 17:4 NKJV

A question that is often asked of the rich and famous is, "How would you like to be remembered?" Before Jesus was crucified, His prayer to His Father reveals to us how He would have answered that question. Jesus' focus would not have been upon Himself, but upon His Father.

The words in Jesus' prayer recorded in John's gospel reveal to us how each person should seek to live and plan to die. There is no greater way to be remembered than to be someone who has glorified God and completed the work that He has given you to do.

Jesus made it clear, that for Him, life was all about pleasing the One who sent Him and leaving nothing undone that His Father asked Him to do.

Everything God Desires for You

"I pray for them. I do not pray for the world
but for those whom You have given Me,
for they are Yours. And all Mine are Yours,
and Yours are Mine, and I am glorified in them."

John 17:9-10 NKJV

Isn't it wonderful to know that the reason Jesus has prayed for you and is praying for you is because you belong to Him. Jesus is not praying for you as His enemy, but as His friend, and as a child in His Father's family.

In His prayers for you, Jesus desires everything for you that His Father desires. There is not a single desire in the heart of God that is not on the lips of Jesus as He prays for you.

Roy Lessin

The Beauty of God's Presence

"Now I am no longer in the world, but these are in the world, and I come to You. Holy Father, keep through Your name those whom You have given Me, that they may be one as We are."

John 17:11 NKJV

Because God wants to bless you, Jesus' prayers for you are filled with blessing. Because God wants to be glorified through your life, Jesus is praying that the Holy Spirit will strengthen you to make the choices that will please the Father. Because God wants you to know Him, Jesus is praying that you will go deeper and deeper into the heart of the Father's love.

Jesus is praying that you be kept from all evil, from all that will rob you of His joy, from all that will keep you from fellowship with Him, and from any disunity with other members of the body of Christ. He is also praying that you will know the beauty of His presence as He shines upon you in true sanctification and holiness.

Be Bold in Prayer

*"Call to Me, and I will answer you, and show you
great and mighty things, which you do not know."*

Jeremiah 33:3 NKJV

You can be bold in prayer today because God

- has invited you to come to Him
- has made a way for you to come through Christ.
- welcomes your prayers
- hears your prayers
- puts no limits on your prayers
- receives your prayers as sweet incense
- answers your prayers.

Roy Lessin

October

*Blessed is every one who fears the L*ORD,

who walks in His ways.

Psalm 128:1 NKJV

Transformed by Christ

Therefore we were buried with Him through baptism into death, that just as Christ was raised from the dead by the glory of the Father, even so we also should walk in newness of life.

Romans 6:4 NKJV

Jesus Christ brings you something that is far greater than information, reformation, or alteration. The power of the gospel of Jesus Christ will *transform* you.

- When you received Christ, you didn't receive a better life, but a new life
- You didn't receive new ideas, but a new way of thinking
- You didn't receive new opportunities to improve yourself, but a new kingdom to rule over you
- You didn't receive better tips on how to handle your problems, but a new Master who is able to handle your entire life.

Roy Lessin

A Prayer To Walk in God's Ways

I have hidden Your word in my heart.
Psalm 119:11

Lord, rule my heart, that my heart may rule my feet, my thoughts, my will, and my ways. May my feet bring the words of good news and the message of glad tidings.

May my feet walk upon the imprint of Your footsteps, move at the pace that You are moving, and focus upon the things that Your eyes are fixed upon. Lift me when I stumble, cleanse me when I'm soiled, and heal my every wound.

Be the canopy I need for shade, the hiding place I need for shelter, the shield I need for defense, the sword I need for battle, and the banner I need for victory. Use me as a light to those who are in darkness, as a billow to those whose ember is cooling, and as a flint to those who need Your fire.

The Blessing of God

*Blessed is every one who fears the L*ORD*,*
who walks in His ways.

Psalm 128:1 NKJV

Walking in the Lord's ways
may not have
the approval of the world,
but it will always
have the blessing of God.

Roy Lessin

Walking in God's Ways

Blessed is every one who fears the LORD,
who walks in His ways.

Psalm 128:1 NKJV

There are a multitude of promises and blessings that are given to those who fear Him and walk in His ways – blessings that will impact your work, your ministry, your well-being, your home, your children, and even your grandchildren (see Ps. 128).

- Walking in God's ways means seeking and listening to godly counsel
- It means to completely avoid a pathway of compromise
- It means not taking the things of God lightly
- It means staying away from the shadows of deceit
- It means not having a divided heart
- It means that you are in agreement with His Word and His ways.

It means a walk of faithfulness and trustfulness, righteousness and truthfulness, holiness and happiness, gratefulness and thankfulness.

His Footsteps, My Pathway

The Last Step –
a Glorious Revelation

For You have delivered my soul from death.
Have You not kept my feet from falling, that I
may walk before God in the light of the living?

Psalm 56:13 NKJV

The last step that you take in your earthly walk with God will, by all means, be a glorious revelation! Your last footstep here on earth will –

- bring you to your first footstep in heaven
- bring you out of the realm of mortality and into the realm of immortality
- bring you to the feet of the One you have been following for so many years
- bring you to the place where you shall gaze upon Jesus and see Him face to face
- bring you from the light of earthly things into the dazzling splendor of God's eternal glory
- bring you to the end of your walk of faith and into the heavenly realities that your heart always knew were there.

Roy Lessin

Jesus Christ Becomes a Man

*Jesus said to him, "Foxes have holes and
birds of the air have nests, but the
Son of Man has nowhere to lay His head."*
Matthew 8:20 NKJV

Jesus Christ is God become man. As a man, Jesus had the same needs that we have, but He never carried concern, fear, or worry about His needs. During His years of public ministry Jesus had to eat, but even though He didn't raise His own food, He never worried about where His next meal would come from.

Jesus needed rest, but even though He didn't own a home, He never worried about where He would sleep. Jesus was responsible for taking care of the twelve disciples that He had called to follow Him, but even though He didn't have a bank account, He was never anxious about providing for them.

Jesus faced opposition and persecution from those who hated Him, yet even though He didn't have bodyguards protecting Him, He was never fearful about man keeping Him from doing His Father's will.

His Footsteps, My Pathway

Your Heavenly Father Cares

Seek first the kingdom of God and His righteousness, and all these things shall be added to you.

Matthew 6:33 NKJV

Jesus asks you to take His yoke upon you, to learn of Him, and to follow Him. He wants you to follow Him in the same way that He followed His Father while He was on earth.

He wants you to live without concern, fear, or worry. He wants you to know that His heavenly Father is your heavenly Father.

He wants you to be certain that in the same way that His Father took care of Him, so your heavenly Father will take care of you.

Roy Lessin

Worry vs. Faith

*"And which of you by worrying
can add one cubit to his stature?"*

Luke 12:25 NKJV

Worry is based upon –

- What you can't do.
- What others don't do.
- What resources you don't have.
- What might happen in the future.
- What problems seem impossible to change.

Faith is based upon –

- What God can do.
- What God has promised.
- What resources God has.
- What God has planned.
- What God's power can change.

There Is a Reason

"LORD, who is like You?"
Psalm 35:10 NKJV

God asks you to trust Him because He is trustworthy.

- There is a reason why you should believe God will do good things for you; it is because He is good.
- There is a reason why you should set no limits upon God; it is because God can do all things.
- There is a reason why you should ask God to do mighty things; it is because God is Almighty.
- There is a reason why you should love God with all of your heart; it is because He loves you with all of His.

Roy Lessin

Praise the Lord

Great is the LORD, and greatly to be praised;
and His greatness is unsearchable.

Psalm 145:3 NKJV

- God is the great Redeemer; He lifts you up from every pit of darkness.
- God is the great Strengthener; He builds you up with every word of truth.
- God is the great Encourager; He cheers you up with every touch of comfort.
- God is the great Helper; He holds you up with every outpouring of grace.

The Filter of God's Truth

*We are bound to give thanks to God always
for you, brethren beloved by the Lord, because God
from the beginning chose you for salvation through
sanctification by the Spirit and belief in the truth.*

2 Thessalonians 2:13 NKJV

One of the greatest errors that a follower of Christ can make is to believe something that is a lie. There is a powerful filter that God has given you to keep all lies from settling into your thinking process.

The filter that is available to you is God's truth. When a thought first enters your mind there is an important question you must ask, "Is this thought the truth?" Your answer to this question cannot be based upon your reasoning, because truth transcends reason; your answer cannot be based upon your experiences, because they are too subjective; your answer cannot be based upon your circumstances, because they are always changing.

The answer can only come from God's Word, the revelation of the Holy Spirit, and the testimony of Jesus Christ.

Roy Lessin

Three Important Questions

*I tell the truth in Christ, I am not lying, my
conscience also bearing me witness in the Holy Spirit.*

Romans 9:1 NKJV

In order to have God's truth as the filtering system
for the thoughts that enter your mind, you must receive the truth when it is revealed to you, you must
love the truth as you love the Author of truth, and
you must obey the truth.

The truth will always lead you to the heart of
God. God's Word is the written truth, the Holy
Spirit is the Spirit of Truth, and Jesus is the Living
Truth.

Before you accept a thought as truth, ask yourself these important questions:

• Does the Bible support this thought?
• Does the Holy Spirit bear witness to this thought?
• Does the life and testimony of Jesus Christ stand
  in agreement with this thought?

The Truth of God

"Sanctify them by Your truth. Your word is truth."
John 17:17 NKJV

The truth of God

- confirms the promises of God
- explains the plan of God
- declares the mind of God
- proclaims the will of God
- reflects the glory of God
- affirms the power of God
- reveals the love of God
- heralds the gospel of God
- exalts the Son of God.

Roy Lessin

Some Affirming Truths

God spoke to Moses and said
to him: "I am the LORD."

Exodus 6:2 NKJV

Here are some affirming truths that God wants to speak to your heart today:

I am an almighty God; do not think that I will only answer your prayers for small things.

I am an all-loving God; do not think that I love you only a little.

I am an ever-present God; do not think that you are ever without Me.

I am a delivering God; do not think that there is a burden too great for Me to lift off your shoulder.

I am a compassionate God; do not think that there is anything in your life that I do not care about.

I am a giving God; do not think that I will withhold My provision from you.

I am an abundant God; do not think that My blessings to you are limited.

I am your Father, God; do not think that I will withhold anything good from you, My child.

Unmovable and Unshakeable

And cried with a loud voice, saying, "Salvation to our God which sitteth upon the throne, and unto the Lamb."

Revelation 7:10 KJV

Everything about God and His kingdom is unmovable and unshakeable. His Word, His Spirit, and His Son are the bedrocks of your faith. Heaven and earth may pass away, but His kingdom will remain.

Faith moves you past your rising and falling emotions and declares, "There is something deeper that my heart is resting upon." Faith takes you past the circumstances of life and proclaims, "There is something stronger that my confidence is leaning upon."

Faith rises above the dark days and the rainy days to boldly affirm, "There is something higher that my hope is counting upon." Faith stands in the assurance that God is in control, that He is on His throne, that His Son is at His right hand, and that the Holy Spirit is your guarantee of good things to come.

Roy Lessin

Walk in Continual Peace

Now may the Lord of peace Himself
continually grant you peace in every
circumstance. The Lord be with you all!
2 Thessalonians 3:16 NASB

The only thing that should cause your spirit to lose its rest, that should cause your heart to faint, and that should cause your faith to falter is if you were to discover that God's kingdom had been shaken, that the Holy Spirit had lost His power, and that Jesus Christ had been dethroned.

Since it is impossible for any of these things to ever happen, you can continue to walk in peace today, regardless of what may be happening around you.

A Prayer of Rest

My soul finds rest in God alone;
my salvation comes from Him.

Psalm 62:1

Lord, I thank You today for who You are, for all You do, and for all that You mean to me. You are my hiding place, my dwelling place, and my resting place. I rest in Your love, Your mercy, Your grace; I rest in Your greatness, Your glory, Your goodness; I rest in Your provisions, Your purposes, Your plans; I rest in Your wisdom, Your ways, Your words; I rest in Your righteousness, Your rule, Your reign; I rest in Your nature, Your character, Your majesty. Lord, I thank You that You are greater than my highest understanding of You.

Roy Lessin

The Direction of God's Love

*Now may the Lord **direct your
hearts** into the love of God.*
2 Thessalonians 3:5 NKJV

Regardless of where you may be living or what you
may be doing, there is one overall direction that
God has for your life. The direction that He is taking you is the direction of His love.

When you get up in the morning and ask God
to direct your steps, He will answer your prayer by
directing you into His love.

It is as though God is saying to you, "Yesterday
I directed you into My love, and today I will direct
you a little further and a little deeper into My love.
Each day that follows will be a continuation of your
journey into My love."

God's Protection

The Lord is faithful, and He will
strengthen and protect you from the evil one.

2 Thessalonians 3:3 NASB

One of the ways that God's faithfulness is demonstrated in your life is by His protection. It is true that you have an enemy, but it is also true that the One who protects you from the enemy is greater than the enemy's domain, wiser than his schemes, stronger than his wiles, and mightier than his limited power.

Roy Lessin

Total Commitment

*I beseech you therefore, by the mercies of God,
that you present your bodies a living sacrifice, holy,
acceptable to God, which is your reasonable service.*

Romans 12:1 NKJV

God desires all of your heart to be fully yielded to Him. God does not love you with half of His heart; He does not watch over you with one eye closed; He does not listen to only a certain percentage of your prayers.

When God sent His Son into the world, God didn't tell Jesus to be partially committed to His will. God didn't have His Son embrace only a part of the cross, or only go a part of the distance up Calvary's hill.

When Jesus came to earth He gave His life completely for you, there was no holding back, turning back, or going back in the plan of God or in the obedience of Jesus.

Give Yourself Wholly To God

*"Caleb the son of Jephunneh; he shall see it, and
to him and his children I am giving the land on which
he walked, because **he wholly followed the Lord**."*

Deuteronomy 1:36 NKJV

God's call upon your life is for you to give yourself
wholly to Him to:

- love Him completely
- obey Him fully
- trust Him entirely
- serve Him totally
- enjoy Him thoroughly.

Roy Lessin

Build an Altar for God

Then Noah built an altar to the Lord.
Genesis 8:20 NKJV

Throughout the Scriptures, men of God built altars to God. The altar was a place of sacrifice, consecration, worship, and prayer. An altar was also a "marking point" in the journey of God's people.

When Noah left the Ark, the first thing he did was build an altar; when Abraham heard the promise of God's covenant blessing, he responded by building an altar; when God confirmed His covenant with Isaac, Isaac gratefully built an altar; when Moses saw the victorious hand of God in battle, he built an altar and declared that God was His banner.

The altar is a place where faith expresses its deepest meaning, its greatest devotion, and its highest honor to the One who is worthy of all that we give to Him.

The Altar in Your Heart

The LORD is God, shining upon us. Bring
forward the sacrifice and put it on the altar.
Psalm 118:27 NLT

An altar should be found within the heart of every
believer – an altar where God is honored, where
His mighty works are acknowledged, where His
ownership of our lives is affirmed, and where the
things that we have surrendered to Him are secure-
ly bound.

The altar in your heart is where you acknowledge
that everything in your life has come from God, and
belongs to God. Let your altar be a place where you
offer up a sweet smelling aroma of prayer, a spirit of
constant worship, and a voice of abundant praise.

Let your altar be the place where you offer devotion to Him who has affirmed His promises to you,
showered His blessings upon you, placed His favor
around you, and poured His love within you.

Roy Lessin

Focus on God's Greatness

Now glory be to God! By His mighty power at work within us, He is able to accomplish infinitely more than we would ever dare to ask or hope.

Ephesians 3:20 NLT

There are no limits to what God has in His heart for you.

- When you come to God as an empty vessel, He wants you to be full and overflowing
- When you come to God seeking bread, He wants you to be completely satisfied
- When you come to God thirsting after Him, He wants your thirst to be totally quenched.

The eyes of your faith need to be focused upon God's greatness, while your heart remains fixed upon His love. Your faith must know God's promises and fully trust in them, while your heart must know God's ways and fully follow them.

The Doorway to Complete Happiness

For thus says the LORD God, the Holy One of Israel:
"In returning and rest you shall be saved;
in quietness and confidence shall
be your strength." But you would not.
Isaiah 30:15 NKJV

Sadly, not everyone wants to fully have what God wants to fully give.

If we are not fully persuaded that God has everything we need, is everything we long for, and will be everything we could ever hope for, we will choose to keep back certain parts of our lives from Him.

Full surrender to God not only means that God has your all, it also means that your life is in the hands of the One you were created to know. Full surrender is the doorway to complete happiness.

Roy Lessin

Let Your Life Be ...

"Let your light so shine before men, that they may see your good works and glorify your Father in heaven."

Matthew 5:16 NKJV

- Let your life be a testimony of who God is, rather than a reflection of who you are trying to be.
- Let your life be a testimony to what God can do, rather than a reflection of what you are trying to accomplish.
- Let your life be a testimony of what God will do through someone who simply trusts Him, fully loves Him, and wholly follows His footsteps.

God Fights Your Battles

The LORD will fight for you while you keep silent.
Exodus 14:14 NASB

How blessed you are to have God fight your battles. When God is your defender, you don't have to argue back, fight back, yell back, or talk back to others.

You don't need to "plan out" your arguments to justify your actions. God does not need to use your tongue as His weapon of warfare. Quietness of heart, mind, spirit, and voice will keep you in a place of great peace.

You do not need to defend yourself or justify any of your actions if you are walking in obedience to what God has asked you to do. If your actions are based upon God's calling in your life, it is justification enough. If what you do is being motivated by love, this is reason enough.

Roy Lessin

Jesus Christ, Your Mediator

*For there is one God and one Mediator
between God and men, the Man Christ Jesus.*

1 Timothy 2:5 NKJV

A mediator takes the hand of one party and places it into the hand of another party. A mediator is someone who has one primary aim, and that is to bring peace to a broken relationship.

Jesus Christ is your representative to God, and He is God's representative to you. As your mediator He presents your need of mercy to God, and as God's mediator He extends God's grace to you.

Jesus Christ is the only mediator that you will ever need, for He is the one whose sacrifice on the cross for sin completely satisfied the demands of God's justice and holiness. The only one that you should ever allow to come between you and God is His Son, Jesus Christ.

Serving Spirit-Beings

*But angels are only servants. They are spirits sent
from God to care for those who will receive salvation.*
Hebrews 1:14 NLT

One of the ways that God ministers to you is through
His angels. Angels are not human beings in a glorified state. Angels are a unique and separate creation
of God.

They are not human beings, but spirit-beings.
They report directly to God and receive their orders
from God. They are God's messengers, sent to perform on earth, the things that have been willed by
God in heaven.

Angels are not omnipotent, but they do have
great power; angels are not omnipresent, but they
can move very swiftly; angels are not omniscient,
but they do know things that man does not know.

You are usually not aware of the ministry that
angels are having in your life, but you can be certain
that they are active and are being used by God according to His will.

Roy Lessin

Abundant Fruitfulness

When they came to what is now known as the valley of Eshcol, they cut down a cluster of grapes so large that it took two of them to carry it on a pole between them! They also took samples of the pomegranates and figs.

Numbers 13:23 NLT

God not only wants your life to be fruitful, but to be abundantly so. The God who can turn a desert land into a land of milk and honey, can take the empty places, the dry places, and the barren places of your life and cause them to produce an abundant harvest.

Do not place your trust in the harvest of your life, but upon the Lord of the harvest; do not focus upon the lushness of your fruit, but upon the watchful care of the Husbandman. God is the one who will increase the influence of your ministry and enlarge the fruitfulness of your life.

The fruit that today is small enough to be carried in the hand of a child, will one day become so large, that it will need to be carried upon the shoulders of strong men.

His Footsteps, My Pathway

Fruit for Life

"Abide in Me, and I in you. As the branch cannot bear fruit of itself, except it abide in the vine; no more can ye, except ye abide in Me."

John 15:4 KJV

What kind of fruit does God want you to have in your life?

Good fruit.
Much fruit.
Sweet fruit.
Beautiful fruit.
Excellent fruit.
Multiplied fruit.
Fruit of your faith.
Fruit of your mouth.
Fruit of your hands.
Fruit that will remain.
Fruit of righteousness.
Fruit that will come forth in its season.
Fruit in your youth and fruit in your old age.

Roy Lessin

November

The God of my rock; in Him will I trust:
He is my shield, and the horn of my salvation,
my high tower, and my refuge, my savior.

2 Samuel 22:3 KJV

Someone Else's Role Model

Be an example to the believers in word,
in conduct, in love, in spirit, in faith, in purity.

1 Timothy 4:12 NKJV

Everyone is a role model. A role model is someone who sets an example. The example of each life will influence someone else's life. Here are six ways that your life can impact others for good.

- **Words**: Words bring the seeds of truth that can be planted in the lives of others.
- **Conduct**: Conduct is the compliment to what you say and the testimony that others see.
- **Love**: Love is the loudest proclamation that a heart has been changed.
- **Spirit**: Communion with God creates a hunger in the lives of others to seek the heart of God.
- **Faith**: Daily trust in God is like an arrow that points others to His faithfulness.
- **Purity**: A holy life is a healthy life that testifies to God's pure, healing streams.

Roy Lessin

Words that Express the Heart of God

The godly speak words that are helpful.
Proverbs 10:32 NLT

What is abiding within you will be what comes out of you. When truth abides in you, truth will be spoken by you. Your speech is a reflection of what is taking place in your heart and in your spirit.

The entrance of Jesus' words into your inner-man will bring forth life-giving words to others. The words that you speak have great power for good when they are filled with truth, seasoned with grace, spoken with kindness, permeated with hope, and saturated with love.

Through your words you express your gratitude and reveal your attitude. Your words can help to cheer a heart, heal a wound, restore a relationship, communicate a vision, encourage a life, lift a spirit, build faith, inspire change, impart wisdom, and express the heart of God.

Trust God

The LORD recompense thy work, and a full
reward be given thee of the LORD God of Israel,
under whose wings thou art come to trust.

Ruth 2:12 KJV

God wants you to trust in Him – with all of your heart, in all of your ways, through all of your life. Let your trust be in the Lord when the sun breaks through your window, when it shines brightly overhead at noonday, and when it sets in the evening sky.

Trust Him when there are clouds, when there are shadows, and when nighttime falls. Trust Him during winter's chill, during spring's new life, during summer's heat and storms, and during fall's rapid changes.

Let every blossom be a reminder that God is doing something new within you; let every mountain be a reminder that God is firmly establishing you in His ways; let every towering tree be a reminder that everything within you is reaching out to Him.

Roy Lessin

Do You Really Trust God?

The God of my rock; in Him will I trust:
He is my shield, and the horn of my salvation,
my high tower, and my refuge, my savior.

2 Samuel 22:3 KJV

We cannot add anything to God's power, we cannot increase His wisdom, we cannot supply Him with any new information, and we cannot improve on anything He has done. What God desires from us is not our efforts, but our trust.

When God tells us that He is all sufficient, He will be pleased when we trust Him as our sufficiency; when God tells us that He is our provider, He will be pleased when we trust Him for our provisions; when God tells us that He is our keeper, He will be pleased when we trust Him to keep us.

The question that a believer does not need to ask is, "Lord, are You able?" but rather, "Am I trusting in the Lord's ability to take care of me?"

Your Provider and Keeper

The LORD recompense thy work, and a full reward be given thee of the LORD God of Israel, under whose wings thou art come to trust.

Ruth 2:12 KJV

The blessings that came upon Ruth were the result of her trust in the Lord to be her provider and keeper. Ruth could no longer trust in her husband, because he had died. She could not trust in her husband's wealth, because he left her none.

She would not trust in her former gods, because she forsook them all. She would not trust in her old friends, because she left them all. She could not trust in her mother-in-law, Naomi, because she had nothing.

Ruth's total commitment to Naomi was based upon her complete trust in Naomi's God, the God of Israel. "Ruth said: "For wherever you go, I will go; and wherever you lodge, I will lodge; your people shall be my people, and your God, my God" (Ruth 1:16 NKJV).

Roy Lessin

Trust God for Everything

To those who trust Him ...

- God will protect (2 Sam. 22:31).
- God will deliver (1 Chron. 5:20).
- God will defend (Ps. 5:11).
- God will bless (Ps. 2:12).
- God will save (Ps. 17:7).
- God will not put to shame (Ps. 31:1).
- God will multiply goodness (Ps. 31:19).
- God will make provision (Ps. 37:3).
- God will work on their behalf (Ps. 37:5).
- God will help in time of fear (Ps. 56:3-4).
- God will give a glad heart (Ps. 64:10).
- God will direct their paths (Prov. 3:5-6).
- God will be their strength, their song, and their salvation (Isa. 12:2).

The LORD is my rock,
my fortress and my deliverer.
Psalm 18:2

A Prayer of Trust

Lord, I trust in You. I trust in Your mercy because You are merciful, I trust in Your grace, for You are gracious, I trust in Your goodness for You are good. I trust in Your strength for You are almighty, I trust in Your council for You are wise, I trust in Your compassion for You are love. I trust in the shelter of Your wings, in the shield of Your protection, in the safety of Your surrounding presence. Lord, I trust in You at all times, in all ways, and for all reasons. I trust in You, because what happens to me matters to You, and because my needs are Your concern. Lord, I trust in You, You are my heavenly Father, and I know that You would never do anything unkind or unloving to one of Your children.

I will say of the LORD,
"He is my refuge and my fortress,
my God, in whom I trust."
Psalm 91:2

Roy Lessin

An Affirmation of Trust

We trust in the living God, who is the
Savior of all men, especially of those who believe.
1 Timothy 4:10 NKJV

My trust is in the Lord, the Creator of all things and my Creator. My heart is at rest for I know that God is faithful and that He keeps His promises. Everything about His character is totally dependable and completely reliable. What He has spoken in His Word, He will fulfill. He not only wills to fulfill His Word, but He also has the resources to fulfill it.

In Him I have found my Champion of all champions, my Certainty of all certainties, my Security of all securities. God cannot fail, for love never fails, and God is love. He quiets my spirit and assures me that I am in His hands.

God Is with You

He Himself has said, "I will never
leave you nor forsake you."
Hebrews 13:5 NKJV

You can trust the One who ...

- Created you
- Died for you
- Cares for you
- Intercedes for you
- Loves you
- Accepts you
- Adopted you
- Claims you
- Provides for you
- Watches over you
- Blesses you
- Calls you
- Strengthens you
- Equips you
- Leads you
- Will never leave you

Roy Lessin

There Is No Other God

*"I am the LORD, and there is none else,
there is no God beside Me."*

Isaiah 45:5 KJV

You can trust the One who ...

- Never makes a mistake,
- Never fails,
- Never forgets,
- Never is unkind,
- Never is unjust,
- Never is unholy,
- Cannot lie,
- Keeps His Word,
- Is Lord over all,
- Is Almighty,
- Is your heavenly Father,
- Is the Covenant keeper,
- Is in control,
- Rules over the universe,
- Sits upon His throne,
- Holds everything together,
- Will remain faithful and true.

God Holds Your Future

He that spared not His own Son, but
delivered Him up for us all, how shall He
not with Him also freely give us all things?

Romans 8:32 KJV

There are a thousand reasons why you should trust
God with all of your heart, but just knowing that
God sent His Son to the cross to die for you, is reason enough. Since God allowed His only begotten
Son to suffer and die an agonizing death upon the
cross so that you could be forgiven, how could He
ever fail you in any other way?

If you can trust Him for your eternal destiny,
how can you not trust Him for your entire earthly
journey? Will not the One who is preparing a place
for you in heaven take care of you while you are on
this earth? The God who holds your future is the
God of your daily peace, your daily joy, and your
daily bread.

Roy Lessin

A Clear Conscience

He is the God I serve with a clear conscience.
2 Timothy 1:3 NLT

A clear conscience brings you great spiritual freedom and liberty. Your conscience is given to you from God to help you be sensitive to His ways and His will. A troubled conscience is to your spirit what pain is to your body. Both are a blessing from God.

Without pain you wouldn't have any sense that something is wrong with your body. When your conscience is troubled, it is warning you that you have allowed something to come into your life that shouldn't be there. When this happens, the Holy Spirit points you to the blood of Jesus, for it is here alone where healing, cleansing, and forgiveness can take place.

When your conscience is clear, it sends a joyful message to your spirit saying, "Walk on in joy and freedom, all is well between you and God."

Your Spiritual Heritage

*I call to remembrance the genuine faith that is in you,
which dwelt first in your grandmother Lois and
your mother Eunice, and I am persuaded is in you also.*

2 Timothy 1:5 NKJV

There are so many people who are blessed today because someone in their family walked in the blessing of God. If you have a parent or a grandparent who walked with God, or is walking with God, you are rich indeed. Your life has been greatly enriched by them in many ways.

You have been enriched through their influence upon you; through the example of their journey, through the encouragement of their faith, and through the multitude of prayers that they have offered in your behalf.

If you do not have this blessing in your family line, allow it to begin with you. If you do, your children and grandchildren will one day be able to look back and thank God for the spiritual heritage that you have brought to them.

Roy Lessin

Qualities of the Holy Spirit

For God has not given us a spirit of fear,
but of power and of love and of a sound mind.
2 Timothy 1:7 NKJV

When you received the Holy Spirit you received God's Spirit. What is true of God is true of the Holy Spirit. It is important for you to know what qualities and characteristics the Holy Spirit has brought into your life, and what He has not.

The Holy Spirit has not brought you anything that shies away from the will of God. The Holy Spirit never tells you to draw back or hold back from God. The Holy Spirit knows nothing of fear or timidity. The Holy Spirit is no coward and has no fear of man.

The Holy Spirit has come to you with power and might to supply you with a heavenly dynamo in your spirit. The Holy Spirit moves you on, calls you to stand firm, and to advance boldly in the things of God.

Immortal Light

*Our Savior Jesus Christ, who has
abolished death and brought life and
immortality to light through the gospel.*

2 Timothy 1:10 *NKJV*

Jesus conquered death. He brought light, resurrection life, and the hope of heaven to a dying race. This light, this hope, this immortality, is yours through the gospel of Jesus Christ.

Roy Lessin

Appointed and Anointed

*I was appointed a preacher, an apostle,
and a teacher of the Gentiles.*

2 Timothy 1:11 NKJV

*And you shall take the anointing oil,
pour it on his head, and anoint him.*

Exodus 29:7 NKJV

It is God's will that every appointed person is also an anointed person. No one who serves God is anointed as a result of a self-appointed ministry. There is no anointing on the things that originate with the flesh. God is using your life for His glory, not because you have come up with a plan to do so, but because He has called you to do so.

God's plan for your life becomes your assignment in life, His gifting becomes your equipping, His power becomes your enabling, His Spirit becomes your anointing.

Because God backs up everything in your life that He has ordained, He is the authority behind everything you do, and it is His anointing that makes your work effective.

Your Glorious Treasure

For God, who said, "Let there be light
in the darkness," has made us understand that
this light is the brightness of the glory of
God that is seen in the face of Jesus Christ.

2 Corinthians 4:6 NLT

The treasure of God is the light that is seen upon the face of Jesus Christ. This light is the reflection of God's glory. What has God chosen to do with this treasure? He has chosen to place it inside the vessels of His people through the Holy Spirit.

You have this glorious treasure in you, so that the light of the gospel can go forth to reach others; so that the light of hope can encourage others; so that the light of love can embrace others; so that the light of mercy can restore others; so that the light of truth can free others; so that the light of compassion can heal others; so that the light of grace can bless others.

Roy Lessin

Powerful Repentance

From that time Jesus began to preach, and to say,
"Repent: for the kingdom of heaven is at hand."
Matthew 4:17 KJV

Repentance is a powerful word with a positive result. Jesus commanded repentance because He was proclaiming the kingdom.

The message of Jesus to every life is this, "You are living in darkness, come to My light; you are dead in your sins, come to Me and live; you are drinking out of muddy pools, come to Me and drink living water; you are indulging in things that do not satisfy, come to Me and be made whole; you are living off crumbs, come to Me and eat the bread of life; you are existing on the least, come to Me and delight in the very best; you get things and gather things and yet remain empty, come to Me and be made full.

The Kingdom Manifested Through You

Jesus went about all Galilee, teaching in their synagogues, and preaching the gospel of the kingdom, and healing all manner of sickness and all manner of disease among the people.

Matthew 4:23 KJV

The gospel of the kingdom moves Jesus Christ into the centermost part of your personality, your spirit, and your heart. He cannot be on the fringes of your life and be the King of your life.

When the King and His kingdom enter your life, they come with great power and authority. His government rules you, His words direct you, His love motivates you, His wisdom guides you, His grace frees you, and His heart draws you close to His.

His kingdom has not come to hide within you, but to be manifested through you. You proclaim His kingdom to others by the way you live, by the choices you make, by the attitudes you express, and by the love you demonstrate.

Roy Lessin

The Life, the Spirit, the Truth

*This letter is from Paul, a slave of God and
an apostle of Jesus Christ. I have been sent to bring
faith to those God has chosen and to teach them to know
the truth that shows them how to live godly lives.*

Titus 1:1 NLT

The life of Jesus will always lead you into a godly life.

The Spirit of God is the *Holy* Spirit, and He will always lead you into a holy life. The truth of God is pure and will always lead you into purity of life.

If you want to know if someone has received the truth and is teaching the truth, look at that person's life. The way a person lives will demonstrate what a person really believes.

- If you want to walk in the light, seek the truth
- If you want to make wise choices, know the truth
- If you want to be a godly example, live the truth
- If you want to please the Lord, love the truth.

Live Victoriously

But watch thou in all things, endure afflictions.

2 Timothy 4:5 KJV

It is not God's will for you to be overtaken by trials, but for you to overcome them. God will give you the endurance you need to overcome, if you are willing to endure.

You endure by planting your feet on the foundation of His kingdom, and setting your faith upon the promises of His Word.

To endure means that you will not bail out of the difficulty you are in. God wants you to stick it out, believing that as you follow His footsteps, He will bring you through victoriously.

Roy Lessin

A Prayer of Endurance

*You need to persevere so that when
you have done the will of God,
you will receive what He has promised.*

Hebrews 10:36

Lord, You are my strength, my sanity, my security, my salvation. Your hand upholds me, Your grace sustains me, Your power supports me. Keep my feet moving forward, keep my faith looking upward, keep my hope pointing homeward. Make a roadway through every rugged mountain, make a pathway through every stormy sea, make a highway through every dark valley. I do not put my faith in my own timetable, but in Your perfect plan. Lord, however long it takes, I will trust You. I receive Your grace to endure all things with pleasantness of spirit, calmness of soul, and thankfulness of heart.

Walking in the Perfect Will of God

***And the Word was made flesh,
and dwelt among us,*** *(and we beheld
His glory, the glory as of the only begotten
of the Father,) full of grace and truth.*

John 1:14 KJV

Jesus Christ was God come in the flesh, bringing the character and nature of God into every aspect of life. Jesus came in a human body and with human needs. He walked in the perfect will of God, even when times were difficult.

When facing persecutions and suffering, Jesus endured them; when facing the temptations of life, Jesus resisted them; when facing the attacks of the devil, Jesus overcame them; when it came to the sins of others, Jesus forgave them.

Roy Lessin

The Word among Us

And the Word was made flesh,
and dwelt among us, (and we beheld
His glory, the glory as of the only begotten
of the Father,) **full of grace and truth.**

John 1:14 KJV

- When people had sorrows, Jesus wept for others
- When people had needs, Jesus had compassion for others
- When people shared joys, Jesus celebrated with others
- When people were hungry, Jesus broke bread for others
- When people were sick, Jesus healed others
- When people were bound, Jesus delivered others
- When people were broken, Jesus restored others
- When people were condemned, Jesus forgave others.

The Reality of Life

Jesus said to him, "I am the way, the truth, and the life.
No one comes to the Father except through Me."

John 14:6 NKJV

Jesus came to bring us life. The word "life" also means "reality." Today Jesus lives in you. He is a real Jesus, living in you to reach a real world, with real needs.

People's basic needs haven't changed, and Jesus' power to meet those needs hasn't changed. Today, He will work through you to touch broken lives, to restore broken relationships, and to heal broken hearts.

Roy Lessin

God's Kingdom at Work

"Blessed are the poor in spirit:
for theirs is the kingdom of heaven."

Matthew 5:3 KJV

As God's kingdom works in your life, God does not ask if you are rich enough, strong enough, great enough, or powerful enough to serve Him. The questions that God asks are these:

- Are you small enough for Me to use you?
- Are you dependent enough for Me to be your only resource?
- Are you poor enough to draw upon My riches?
- Are you weak enough to lean on My strength?

His Footsteps, My Pathway

Abba, Father

*For ye have not received the spirit of bondage
again to fear; but ye have received the Spirit
of adoption, whereby we cry, Abba, Father.*

Romans 8:15 KJV

When the Holy Spirit comes to live within you, the deepest cry that He puts within your heart is Abba, Father. God, the Mighty One, the Holy One, the Righteous One, is your Father!

The name, Abba, is an endearing name. It is a name that speaks of closeness, and intimacy. It is the name that a child speaks when he draws close to his father and feels his loving embrace.

Roy Lessin

In the Lord's Strength

Be strong in the Lord and in His mighty power.
Ephesians 6:10

God wants you to be strong in Him.

It is His strength that enables you to face trials, for He is your deliverer.

It is His strength that enables you to walk through dark places, for He is your light; It is His strength that enables you to face sorrow, for He is your comforter.

His strength never weakens, His might never diminishes, His power never fades. You can do everything He calls you to do, because He never asks you to do anything without Him.

A Place of Recovery

So David went, he and the six hundred men
that were with him, and came to the brook Besor,
where those that were left behind stayed.

1 Samuel 30:9 KJV

When David and his men were in pursuit of the Amalekites, they came to the brook Besor. Besor means "cheerful." This brook provided cheer as a place of refreshing for David's tired men. It also provided cheer as a place of recovery for those who were too weary to continue the pursuit of the enemy.

When David had overtaken the Amalekites and defeated them, he returned to the men who had stayed behind at the brook. David brought them cheer by giving them an equal share in the spoils that had been taken from the enemy.

When you are in the midst of spiritual warfare, God has a "brook of Besor" to cheer you. This brook is symbolic of the joy that the Holy Spirit brings to you, and the blessings that are yours as a result of Christ's victory.

Roy Lessin

Joy in Spiritual Battle

*My brethren, count it all joy when
you fall into various trials.*

James 1:2 NKJV

The presence of a spiritual battle does not mean that you need to experience the absence of joy.

- Rejoice to the extent that you partake of Christ's sufferings, that when His glory is revealed, you may also be glad with exceeding joy (1 Pet. 4:13 NKJV).
- And you became followers of us and of the Lord, having received the word in much affliction, with joy of the Holy Spirit (1 Thess. 1:6 NKJV).
- Looking unto Jesus, the author and finisher of our faith, who for the joy that was set before Him endured the cross, despising the shame, and has sat down at the right hand of the throne of God (Heb. 12:2 NKJV).

December

"At that moment you will know absolutely that I'm in My Father, and you're in Me, and I'm in you."

John 14:20 MSG

Roy Lessin

Jesus' Great Love for You

*But God commendeth His love toward us, in that,
while we were yet sinners, Christ died for us.*

Romans 5:8 KJV

The calendar tells you *when* Jesus died upon the cross for your sins.

The city of Jerusalem tells you *where* Jesus was crucified for your sins.

The agony of the cross tells you *what* it was like for Jesus to be crucified for your sins.

The nailing of Jesus' body to the cross tells you *who* was crucified for your sins.

But, to understand the reason *why* Jesus was crucified for your sins, you must understand His great love for you.

Yesterday, Today and For Ever the Same

Jesus Christ the same
yesterday, and today, and for ever.
Hebrews 13:8 KJV

When your life is in Jesus' hands, you are in a safe and secure place. He will not be for you one minute and against you the next; He will not be with you one moment and gone the next; He will not give you rest one day and let you struggle the next. Jesus is the promise maker, the promise giver, and the promise keeper.

Jesus is more certain than the sun in the sky and the ground that is under your feet. Jesus won't age or grow feeble; He won't become out of date or out of touch; He won't lose His power or be stripped of His authority. Jesus' reign and rule are the most certain things in the universe, and your life couldn't be in better hands.

Roy Lessin

Jesus Christ Never Changes

Jesus Christ the same
yesterday, and today, and for ever.
Hebrews 13:8 KJV

People change all the time. One day someone is in power, the next day he is out of power; one day someone makes a promise, the next day that promise is broken; one day someone is your friend, the next day that person is your enemy.

Isn't it good to know that when you read the newspaper or listen to the news, you will never hear a headline that states, "There's something different to report about Jesus." Jesus Christ never changes. Who He is, is who He was. Who He was, is who He will always be.

There are no shocks or surprises in Jesus' character, in His person, or in His position. His heart is the same, His love is the same, His glory is the same, His faithfulness is the same, and His promises are the same.

Jesus Will Provide

"I am the vine, you are the branches. He who abides in Me, and I in him, bears much fruit; for without Me you can do nothing."

John 15:5 NKJV

Jesus said that without Him you could do nothing, but that also means that with Him you can do all things. When He asks you to speak for Him, He will give you the words; when He asks you to follow Him, He will give you the direction; when He asks you to bless others, He will provide the resources needed.

Roy Lessin

Jesus Is Joined To Your Life

"At that moment you will know absolutely that I'm in My Father, and you're in Me, and I'm in you."

John 14:20 MSG

Jesus never wants you to be isolated from Him or to be independent of Him. Jesus is joined to your life in a way that is closer than any person and dearer than any friend.

Jesus said, "I am in the Father." That means that Jesus is as close to the Father as He can possibly be.

Jesus said, "You are in Me." That means that you are as close to the Father as Jesus is. It also means that you are as close to Jesus as you can possibly be.

What Jesus said about your closeness to Him goes even deeper, because He also said, "I am in you." That means that Jesus is as close to you as He can possibly be.

A Prayer of Closeness

Jesus, You are my life. You are the reason I live. You are my gladness and my song of songs. You are closer to me than my very breath, for You have joined Your spirit to my spirit. You know me at my deepest level, and I know that You are revealing Yourself to me at the deepest level of Your being. I abide in You, I am one with You. You are the subject of my thoughts, the heartbeat of my affections, the center of my motivations, the object of my aspirations, and the fulfillment of all my heart knows to be true.

Draw near to God and He
will draw near to you.
James 4:7 NKJV

Roy Lessin

An Affirmation of Closeness

You belong to the Lord. You are His possession. He is your Father and you are His child. He is the Father of all fathers to you. He loves you with a perfect love. He is also your truest friend.

Your identity is in Him. Your confidence is in Him. Your covering is in Him. He knows and understands your heart. Because He is your Father you are secure in His arms and have no fear about your future.

He cares for you, and in complete faithfulness, He instructs you with unfailing wisdom. He orders your steps, and He teaches you His ways. He gives you good gifts and encourages you to do what pleases Him.

"I am with you always,
even to the end of the age."
Matthew 28:20 NKJV

Whatever Things are True

*Finally, brethren, **whatever things are true,**
whatever things are noble, whatever things
are just, whatever things are pure, whatever things
are lovely, whatever things are of good report,
if there is any virtue and if there is anything
praiseworthy – meditate on these things.*

Philippians 4:8 NKJV

- There is no reason to ever think you are alone – God has sent His heavenly host to surround you and work in your behalf in unseen ways.
- There is no reason to ever think you are defense-less – God has a perfect defense for every attack of the enemy, and your shield of faith will block every enemy arrow.
- There is no reason to ever think you are inad-equate – God is your sufficiency, and He will never come up short in His care for you.
- There is no reason to ever think you are use-less – God is daily unfolding the plans He has for you, and those plans include using you for His glory.

Roy Lessin

Medidate on These Things

Finally, brethren, whatever things are true,
whatever things are noble, whatever things
are just, whatever things are pure, whatever things
are lovely, whatever things are of good report,
if there is any virtue and if there is anything
*praiseworthy – **meditate on these things.***

Philippians 4:8 NKJV

- There is no reason to ever think you are empty – God has sent His Holy Spirit into your life to fill you with heaven's richest blessings.
- There is no reason to ever think you are inferior – God has gifted you according to His will and given you grace and faith to fulfill His plan for your life.
- There is no reason to ever think you are hopeless – God will never give up on you as He shapes you into the image of His Son.
- There is no reason to ever think you are unaccepted – God has accepted you with open arms and with an all-embracing love.

Scriptures of Closeness

He shall cover you with His feathers,
and under His wings you shall take refuge;
His truth shall be your shield and buckler.

Psalm 91:4 NKJV

How great is the love the Father has
lavished on us, that we should be called
children of God! And that is what we are!

1 John 3:1

The LORD is near to all who call upon
Him, to all who call upon Him in truth.

Psalm 145:18 NKJV

For I am persuaded that neither death nor life, nor
angels nor principalities nor powers, nor things present
nor things to come, nor height nor depth, nor any
other created thing, shall be able to separate us from
the love of God which is in Christ Jesus our Lord.

Romans 8:38-39 NKJV

Roy Lessin

A Light and Easy Burden

"My yoke is easy, and my burden is light."
Matthew 11:30 KJV

Even though the circumstances you are walking through may be difficult and the burden may be great, Jesus' yoke upon you will be easy and His burden will be light. His will for you during hard times is never retreat or defeat, but steadfastness and patient endurance.

- His promise of "lightness" means that there will always be hope where He is present
- There will always be encouragement where His voice is heard
- There will always be comfort where He is called upon
- There will always be victory where His Spirit dwells
- There will always be fruit where His presence abides
- There will always be grace where His mercies are extended
- There will always be love where His heart is known.

Hold On To Hope

*Hold fast the confidence and the
rejoicing of the hope firm to the end.*

Hebrews 3:6 NKJV

There are some things that God wants you to hold
on to and to never release your grip upon. They include the confidence that you have in Him, and the
certainty of the hope that you have received from
Him.

Take possession of what you possess in God,
lock them in your heart, and throw away the key.
You should never let your confidence in God's
goodness and your hope in His faithfulness ever
slip away because of anything you may question or
not understand.

Keep on your journey, keep following His footsteps, and keep trusting His Word with every confidence.

Roy Lessin

The Starting Point

*For it was fitting for Him, for whom are
all things and by whom are all things, in
bringing many sons to glory, to make the captain
of their salvation perfect through sufferings.*

Hebrews 2:10 NKJV

God wants you to shine with His radiance, to live in
His presence, and to partake of His eternal delights.
He has made it possible, through His Son, for you to
be where He is, to live as He lives, and to know Him
as He knows you.

His will for you upon this earth is only the starting point. You will have to wait until you get to
heaven to fully discover the glorious unfolding of
His will for your life.

The Newness of Life

*But God forbid that I should glory, save in
the cross of our Lord Jesus Christ, by whom the
world is crucified unto me, and I unto the world.*

Galatians 6:14 KJV

One of the reasons that we can glory in the cross
is because, although it is the place of death, it also
leads us to newness of life. God calls us to come to
the cross and die, but His call does not end there.
*The empty tomb is the completed message of the occupied
cross.*

When God asks you to come to the cross to put
something down, He will also direct you to pick
something up. God will ask you to place your own
way upon the cross, but He will also ask you to pick
up His plans and purposes for your life.

He will ask you to die to the world, but He will
ask you to pick up Kingdom realities.

Roy Lessin

Knowing God's Heart

They have not known My ways.

Hebrews 3:10 NKJV

God not only wants you to see His works of greatness, but He also wants you to know the ways of His heart. To know God's *works* means that you know Him at a distance through observation. To know God's *ways* means that you know Him personally through intimacy.

God not only wants you to know the works of His hands, but He also wants you to know the ways of His heart. To know His works means to know what He is doing; to know His heart means to know what He is thinking and feeling.

Knowing His heart means understanding what is important to Him and living with His approval. Knowing His heart means coming into His peace, His righteousness, His joy, and most of all, into His love.

Complete in Christ

*For in Him dwells **all the fullness** of the
Godhead bodily; and you are complete in Him,
who is the head of all principality and power.*

Colossians 2:9-10 NKJV

Nothing needs to be added to Jesus' person or position to make Him more complete. Because He is the fullness of the Godhead bodily, He does not need to be or have anything else. Because He is the head of the church, He does not need to receive more authority. Because He has all power, He does not need to receive more strength.

When Jesus comes into your life, you have received completeness. If you were an empty house, He would be the complete furnishing; if you were an empty plate, He would be the complete meal. If you were a violin, He would be the symphony, if you were a book cover, He would be the manuscript, if you were a vase, He would be the floral arrangement.

Roy Lessin

Jesus' Completeness Makes You Complete

*For in Him dwells all the fullness of the Godhead bodily; and **you are complete** in Him, who is the head of all principality and power.*

Colossians 2:9-10 NKJV

It takes Jesus' completeness to make a complete you – not a degree, not a position, not power, not wealth, not amusement, not property, not beauty, not environment, not sport, not popularity – but Jesus!

Drawing Near with Confidence

Let us therefore draw near with confidence
to the throne of grace, that we may receive mercy
and may find grace to help in time of need.

Hebrews 4:16 NASB

As you follow God's footsteps, His voice will always be calling your heart to draw near to Him. "Come close," will be His call to you. You will never hear Him say to you, "Stay away. Turn away, Go away."

As you do come and draw close to Him, you will hear Him say, "Come closer still. Come closer to My mercies, come closer to My grace, come closer to My heart."

Roy Lessin

The Lord Is Gracious

He has made His wonders to be remembered;
the LORD is gracious and compassionate.

Psalm 111:4 NASB

How good and gracious God is to you. How kind and abundant is His generosity to you. When you were in your darkest night of sin, God brought you into His light; when you were in spiritual poverty, God brought you the riches of His grace; when you were in spiritual loneliness, God brought you the fellowship of His Son; when you were exposed before Him in the nakedness of your sins, He wrapped you in robes of righteousness; when your heart was broken and your life was filled with pain, He comforted you and wiped away your tears; when you were homeless and hopeless, far away from the Father's heart, He drew you near and promised you an eternal home with Him, in His house, forever.

The Signs God Gives

God also bearing witness both with signs and
wonders, with various miracles, and gifts
of the Holy Spirit, according to His own will?

Hebrews 2:4 NKJV

The signs that God now gives – the wonders that God performs, the miracles that God manifests, the gifts that God imparts – confirm to us the glorious truth of the Gospel, the power of the resurrection of Jesus Christ, and the authority that is in His mighty name.

The Babe of Bethlehem is now the ascended and exalted King of kings and Lord of lords. The One who was once in a manger, is now seated at His Father's right hand. The One who once yielded to Roman rule, now rules over all things in heaven and earth.

Roy Lessin

Jesus, Savior of the World

*And we have seen and do testify that the
Father sent the Son to be the Savior of the world.*
1 John 4:14 KJV

Jesus is historical, but He is not an out-of-date
Savior. He is

- at the right hand of the Father, but He is not a
  distant Savior
- holy and righteous, but He is not an unapproach-
  able Savior
- tender and meek, but He is not a soft Savior
- patient and kind, but He is not a passive Savior
- compassionate and forgiving, but He is not a
  permissive Savior
- understanding and merciful, but He is not a
  compromising Savior
- strong and mighty, but He is not a harsh Savior
- coming again, but He is not a far-off Savior.

The Living Word

And the Word was made flesh, and dwelt among us,
(and we beheld His glory, the glory as of the
only begotten of the Father,) full of grace and truth.

John 1:14 KJV

The Son of God is the Word of God. He is the Living Word – the Word of power, the Word of glory, and the Word of creation. God wants us to know the Word, because in knowing the Word we know God. God wanted us to be able to see Him with our eyes and touch Him with our hands. In order to do this, God sent the Word into our world.

The Word took on human flesh and came to live among us. God did this because He wants us to listen to His Son (The Word) and know what God desires for us; God wants us to watch His Son and know what God wants to demonstrate to us; God wants us to follow His Son and know what God destined for us.

Roy Lessin

Glory To God

You will hear the voice of an angel of the Lord proclaiming to a small band of shepherds the following good news, "Have I got something to say to you! It's news that is too good *not* to be true. It's news that will flood you with joy from your head to your toes. God has done it! He has sent the One that He has promised to send, the Jewish Messiah, from David's very seed. Yes, it is Yeshua, God's Salvation, who has come to save you from your sins."

The news was so exciting that a huge number of angels could no longer contain themselves. In one thunderous voice they shouted out, "Glory, glory to God in heaven's highest place. He has sent to earth's lowly place His gift of perfect peace, and it is now available for all who will believe."

Paraphrased from Luke 2

Excitement and Celebration (I)

Suddenly a great company of the heavenly host appeared with the angel, praising God.

Luke 2:13

Why did the angels have such excitement and celebration? We only need to know the names that belong to Jesus to understand why.

- *Jesus* – the One who saves you from your sins and who brings you forgiveness from the past.
- *Christ* – the One sent by God for you; the Messiah, the fulfillment of every promise God has made to you in His Word; the only One anointed by God to redeem you.
- *Immanuel* – the One who came from heaven to earth to bring you from earth to heaven; God living in the midst of your life, being with you, and abiding in you.

Roy Lessin

Excitement and Celebration (II)

- *The Word* – the One who formed you in your mother's womb, brought you into existence, and created you for His eternal purpose.
- *Dayspring* – the One who brought light to your darkness – bringing you the hope of a new day, a new beginning, and a new life.
- *Wonderful* – the One who does wondrous things for you, good things to you, and beautiful things within you.
- *Prince of Peace* – the One who quiets your heart, calms your spirit, and brings rest to your soul.
- *Counselor* – the One who guides your footsteps, leads you in the paths of righteousness, and speaks the love of the Father to your heart.

To us a child is born,
to us a son is given.
And He will be called
Wonderful Counselor, Mighty God,
Everlasting Father, Prince of Peace.
Isaiah 9:6

Celebrate the Gift of Salvation

*But when the kindness of God our Savior
and His love for mankind appeared, He saved us.*

Titus 3:4-5 NASB

*He saved us, not on the basis of deeds
which we have done in righteousness, but
according to His mercy, by the washing of
regeneration and renewing by the Holy Spirit.*

Titus 3:5 NASB

*Whom He poured out upon us
richly through Jesus Christ our Savior.*

Titus 3:6 NASB

*That being justified by His grace we might be
made heirs according to the hope of eternal life.*

Titus 3:7 NASB

Roy Lessin

Faith in God

*When Jesus heard it, He marveled, and said to
those who followed, "Assuredly, I say to you, I have
not found such great faith, not even in Israel!"*

Matthew 8:10 NKJV

As you follow God's pathway, He wants your faith
in Him to be strong and to grow even stronger. You
can never trust Him too much or too often. God
wants you to walk by faith and to live by faith.

He wants you to have faith in who He is and in
what He can do. He wants you to have faith in Him
for what He has prepared for you in heaven, and He
wants you to have faith in Him for your day to day
needs here on earth.

When Jesus walked among men, He experienced
little joy when He saw others respond to Him with
little faith; however, Jesus also experienced great
joy when He saw others respond to Him with great
faith.

Counting the Cost

And Simon answering said unto Him, "Master, we have toiled all the night, and have taken nothing: nevertheless at thy word I will let down the net."

Luke 5:5 KJV

Saying "nevertheless" does not mean that you have said "no" to God. Saying "nevertheless" can mean that you have heard what God has said, you have reflected upon what He has said, and you have counted the cost of what it will mean to do what He has said.

Saying "nevertheless" can mean that you have considered other options, but have chosen to put those aside and follow God's direction. There will be times when following God's will can mean facing a difficult trial, nevertheless, you move on in trust.

There will be times when your reasoning tells you not to do what God is asking, nevertheless, you take a step of faith. There may be times when all you see is darkness, nevertheless, you continue on in hope.

Roy Lessin

Walk in Faith

Thy word is a lamp unto my feet,
and a light unto my path.
Psalm 119:105 KJV

Following God's footsteps will always be a walk of faith. God reveals the pathway that He has for your life, one step at a time. The light that He shines upon your pathway is like a lantern that reveals what is at your feet, not what is five miles down the path.

God has not made your journey of faith complicated. His footsteps do not go in ten different directions. When God shows you your next step, don't erase it, avoid it, pretend you didn't see it, or look for an alternative route. What are you to do today? Simply take the next the step of obedience.

His Footsteps, My Pathway

Perfect Peace

"For Thou hast delivered my soul from death:
wilt not Thou deliver my feet from falling, that I
may walk before God in the light of the living?"

Psalm 56:13 KJV

Following the Lord's footsteps keeps you from
stumbling about or walking in confusion. As you
face a new year, your steps are guided by the One
who goes before you and prepares the way. He leads
you gently like a shepherd leads his sheep. He sets
the perfect pace for you. He knows when it is time
to move ahead and when it is time to rest.

As He leads you, He straightens the crooked
places and makes the rough places smooth. You can
begin each day by committing it to Him, knowing
that He will lead you in the paths of peace and direct your steps into what is good and right. As you
walk in His ways and follow His footsteps, you will
not live a life of regrets.

Roy Lessin

Choose the Best Life

Come, and let us go up to the mountain of the LORD,
to the house of the God of Jacob; He will teach us
His ways, and we shall walk in His paths.

Micah 4:2 NKJV

As you daily choose to make God's footsteps your pathway, you have chosen to live the best life you could possibly live.

His Footsteps, My Pathway